THE NATIONAL TRUST

Desk Diary

1999

THE NATIONAL TRUST

Published in Great Britain in 1998
The National Trust (Enterprises) Ltd, 36 Queen Anne's Gate
London SW1H 9AS

Registered Charity no. 205846

ISBN 0 7078 0254 7

FRONT COVER: Detail from a late sixteenth-century cushion at Hardwick Hall depicting Winter, with the fowler returning home with the birds he has caught. Embroidered figures, trees and even a little fishing pavilion are applied to a black velvet background. *(NTPL/John Hammond)*

BACK COVER: Tiger-head finial from the golden throne of Tipu Sultan, now in the Clive Indian Museum at Powis Castle. *(NTPL/Erik Pelham)*

Articles by Margaret Willes, Publisher, The National Trust

Picture Research by Margaret Willes and Sophie Blair

Designed by Humphrey Stone

Astronomical information reproduced, with permission, from data produced by HM Nautical Almanac Office
© Particles Physics and Astronomy Research Council

Phototypeset in Monotype Sabon Series 669
by SPAN Graphics Ltd, Crawley, West Sussex (SG1289)

Printed by Tien Wah Press Ltd,
Singapore

THE SNOWSHILL COSTUME COLLECTION

The National Trust has provided a facility to enable scholars to study items from the Snowshill Collection that are currently held in store at Berrington Hall, Herefordshire (see pp.10–12). Anyone wishing to pursue this should write to the Assistant Historic Buildings Representative, The National Trust Severn Regional Office, Mythe End House, Tewkesbury, Gloucestershire GL20 6EB specifying the articles they would like to see and giving details of their research purpose. All visits must be organised in advance. The Trust intends to put some of the garments from the Snowshill Collection on display when funds are available and a suitable building can be found.

Introduction

The theme of this year's diary is National Trust collectors. It has proved a rich vein to tap as there are many connected with the Trust, and within their ranks are some fascinating and colourful characters whose acquisitive passions for anything from books, beds and boats to plants, paintings and pewter span the centuries.

The collections featured here range from the deliberate – of paintings and sculpture by Lord Egremont at Petworth; of costume, by Charles Paget Wade and Paulise de Bush, now at Berrington and Killerton – to the more accidental: the Clive Indian Collection at Powis, fruits of the spoils of war; and the state beds and furniture at Knole acquired through the perks enjoyed by Charles Sackville, 6th Earl of Dorset, as Lord Chamberlain. Nor are they all contents of houses: there is the the natural history collection built up by the Harpur Crewes that extends into the grounds of Calke Abbey; the exotic plants collected first by intrepid plant hunters, and then by the Batemans at Biddulph Grange; and Beatrix Potter's collection of hill farms which has done so much to preserve the traditional way of life of the Lake District.

Are collectors born, or do they develop the habit? Charles Paget Wade and James Bateman both relate how their passion for collecting began in their childhood. Bess of Hardwick and Maggie Greville may have lived over three centuries apart, but their stories contain interesting parallels: early setbacks not only made them tough ladies to deal with, but also gave them the determination to surround themselves with collections of the good things of life – good things that we are still enjoying.

I am grateful for all the help I have been given by my colleagues at the National Trust, and to Santina Levey for her splendid introduction to the Hardwick textiles, now published as *An Elizabethan Inheritance*.

While I was compiling this diary, we learnt of the death of James Lees-Milne. As Secretary to the Historic Buildings Committee, he persuaded many owners that their houses – and collections – should pass to the care of the National Trust. In his diaries he painted wonderfully vivid portraits of some of the people behind those collections. He will be much missed.

Margaret Willes, Publisher, 1998

Preserving a Way of Life

In 1905 Beatrix Potter bought Hill Top at Near Sawrey, the first of her collection of Lake District farms. At the time she wrote, 'My purchase seems to be regarded as a huge joke.' This defensiveness may well have stemmed from the overbearing attitude of her rather stuffy parents, who certainly did not approve of their daughter branching out in this independent manner.

Beatrix Potter had been introduced to the Lake District in 1882 when her father Rupert abandoned his usual holiday destination of Scotland and took Wray Castle on Lake Windermere for the summer. Not only did she become entranced by the beauty of the place and the 'quaint, old fashioned people' but she had also noted the concerns for the preservation of the landscape and of the traditional Lake District way of life voiced by Hardwicke Rawnsley, Vicar of Wray, later one of the founders of the National Trust, and a close family friend.

Hill Top was a working farm of 34 acres, which Beatrix Potter was able to buy with a small legacy and royalties earned from her little books of children's stories, notably *The Tale of Peter Rabbit*, published in 1902 and enjoying tremendous success. Although she continued to live in London, she paid regular visits, staying in the old farmhouse while her farm manager, John Cannon, lived with his family in an extension that she designed and had built. Life at Hill Top provided the backdrop for the stories that she wrote in the next few years. Many of her characters were based on the animals there, notably Mrs Tabitha Twitchit, her son Tom Kitten, Jemima Puddle-Duck, and the 'dreadful 'normous big rat', Mr Samuel Whiskers.

Four years later, Beatrix Potter bought her second farm in Sawrey: Castle Farm. She was helped in this purchase by a local solicitor from Hawkshead, William Heelis. Business gradually developed into romance, and Heelis and Beatrix were married in October 1913, moving into Castle Cottage and leaving Hill Top as a typical Lake District farmhouse, a study and a place to entertain the increasing number of visitors inspired by her books.

With her marriage, Beatrix Potter passed into a new existence, which she described in 1925 to Miss Bertha Mahony of the Boston Bookshop, who wanted a few lines for her many supporters in the United States:

Beatrix Potter when she was President of the Keswick Show, 1935. (NT)

Beatrix Potter is Mrs William Heelis. She lives in the North of England, her

> home is amongst the mountains and lakes that she has drawn in her picture books. Her husband is a lawyer. They have no family. Mrs Heelis is in her sixtieth year. She leads a very busy contented life, living always in the country and managing a large sheep farm on her own land.

By this time her eyesight was troubling her: she found she had lost the faculty for seeing clear colours, so her output of illustrated books was declining rapidly. Instead she threw herself into her farming activities. In 1924 she bought Troutbeck Farm at the head of Troutbeck Valley, 1,900 acres for sheep grazing rising up towards Kirkstone Pass. As a life member of the National Trust, she recognised the urgency of securing a deal to prevent the estate going to developers keen to build houses in the valley bottom.

Beatrix Potter offered to pass on Troutbeck Farm to the Trust at her death, making certain stipulations which show how important she considered the conservation of the traditional way of life. First, the estate had to be kept in its entirety, with a 'good intelligent, solvent tenant preferable to a rack rent'. Another condition was that the traditional furniture be retained in the farmhouse, as 'Lakes housewives are accustomed to the care of old oak furniture'. For many years she had attended local auctions of furniture, keeping a record of what she saw as distinctive features of traditional pieces, such as the Coniston cupboard.

A third stipulation was that pure Herdwick sheep should continue to be stocked on the farm. A breed indigenous to the Lake District, Herdwicks are small and hardy with coarse dark wool suited to the harsh fell climate. By the 1920s they were under threat because farmers preferred softer fleeces and more productive lambs. When the tenants moved out of Troutbeck, Beatrix decided to run the farm herself, choosing Tom Storey as her first shepherd. Together they built up a celebrated flock of Herdwicks at Hill Top and in the 1930s won all the prizes for ewes at local shows.

Beatrix's final addition to her collection of Lake District farms was perhaps the most dramatic: purchase of the Monk Coniston estate, in all over 4,000 acres by Coniston Water. This included Monk Coniston Hall, the famous beauty spot of Tarn Hows, seven farms, cottages and open fell. She offered to sell on part of the estate to the Trust when the necessary money had been raised, retaining the rest with the intention that it should pass to the Trust at her death. The Trust readily accepted this arrangement, asking her to manage the farms on their behalf.

Thus began an interesting relationship, for in the years that followed, her views, practical and strongly held, often set her at odds with the organisation. Of the repair of one of the farms on the Monk Coniston estate, she wrote:

> The mason Cookson and his labourers have been most conscientious in their

> work doing it old fashioned style . . . I can only say if I have spent too much I am totally unrepentant. I consider Yew Tree as a typical north-country farmhouse, very well worth preserving. Besides, you cannot let a farm without a habitable house.

The Trust's agent for the Lake District, Bruce Thompson, raised her particular ire. His destruction of some fine oaks offended her artist's eye: 'it is impossible to inculcate a pictorial sense of trees arranged in landscape, when imagination is a blank.'

Thompson was also the subject of her most devastating remark, 'The Trust is a noble thing, and – humanly speaking – immortal. There are some silly mortals connected with it; but they will pass.' This philosophical view prevailed, and when Beatrix Potter died in December 1943, she left her 15 farms, many cottages and 4,000 acres of land to her husband Willy, instructing that they should pass at his death to the National Trust.

Perks of the Job

Vita Sackville-West, writing of her ancestors in *Knole and the Sackvilles*, described Charles Sackville, who became 6th Earl of Dorset in 1677, as 'the most jovial and debonair figure in the Knole picture gallery'. When Charles II was restored to his throne in 1660, Sackville was a young man in his late teens. By rank, wealth and disposition he was made for the Restoration Court and took up its delights with gusto. His mistress was the orange girl turned actress 'pretty, witty Nell Gwynn', whom he inherited from the dramatist Charles Hart before she moved on into the King's bed. Thereafter she always referred to Sackville as her Charles the Second, and the King as Charles the Third.

Sackville was also a poet and patron of the arts, numbering amongst his friends and protégés dramatists such as Congreve, Wycherley and Otway, and poets such as Dryden, Lord Rochester, Prior and Pope. Matthew Prior described Sackville's hospitality in the Poets' Parlour at his country house, Knole in Kent: 'a freedom reigned at his table which made every one of his guests think himself at home'. On one of these evenings of merriment guests were invited to write a few lines in a competition to be judged by Dryden. The host's contribution was pronounced the best, for it read 'I promise to pay Mr John Dryden five hundred pounds on demand. Signed Dorset.' Dryden's verdict was 'that I am equally charmed with the style and the subject'.

Charles Sackville, 6th Earl of Dorset, in a portrait painted by Sir Godfrey Kneller in 1706. Kneller depicts him in damask dressing gown and fur turban, informal attire which he might have worn to entertain his literary friends in the Poets' Parlour at Knole. (NTPL)

Lord Dorset could afford this lavish generosity because he inherited wealth, particularly from his mother, Frances Cranfield, heiress to the Earl of Middlesex. He was also rich through his connections at court. In 1668 he became Groom of the Bedchamber to Charles II, which gave him private access to the King. The following year he went to France as ambassador to the court of Louis XIV and helped to negotiate the secret Treaty of Dover. This privileged status was only imperilled on Charles II's death and his brother James's succession to the throne in 1685, for the new king was no friend of Sackville's. But his luck held, for James II fled the country in December 1688 leaving his daughter Mary to become joint consort with her Dutch husband, William III. Dorset was given the immensely powerful and lucrative post of Lord Chamberlain, the man responsible for the 'above stairs' running of the royal palaces, principally Whitehall, Kensington and Hampton Court.

The duties of this position included arranging the accommodation of the court as it moved from palace to palace, and accompanying the King on his frequent visits to Holland. But the opportunities would be more than just compensation for these onerous responsibilities: Dorset could sell public offices and provide for those who sought patronage. A letter of complaint allegedly found pinned on the Lord Chamberlain's door offers an interesting contrast to the verses of adulation penned by his friends in the Poets' Parlour:

> If Papist, Jew or Infidel
> Would buy a place at Court
> Here Dorset lives, the Chamberlain
> To whom you may resort.
> Then come away, make no delay
> Bring coin to plead your cases.
> He'll turn the King's friends out of doors
> And put you in their places.

The other great benefit of his post as Lord Chamberlain was that he could claim as perquisites, or the perks of his job, the disposal of furniture from the palaces either on the death of the sovereign or when such furniture and furnishings were deemed to be out of date. This was a particularly good time for perquisites, as William and Mary not only had very different taste in interior decoration and style of living from James II, but with the death of Queen Mary in 1694, her husband sought to distance himself from the trappings of the Stuart kings.

From Whitehall and Hampton Court, therefore, came the collection of upholstered and carved seventeenth-century furniture which is now one of the glories of Knole. In the King's Room is the furniture probably designed by Louis XIV's upholsterer Jean Peyrard in 1673 for the marriage of James, then Duke of York, to Mary of Modena. The magnificent state bed was recorded as 'rich gold and silver ... lined with cherry coloured satin embroidered complete'. The accompanying chairs and stools are appropriately carved with *amorini* with bows and quivers and billing doves. Another bed belonging to James, this time made for him when he was King in 1688 by Thomas Roberts, is in the Venetian Ambassador's Room. The richly carved and gilded bed with hangings of blue-green Genoa velvet is again accompanied by a set of two armchairs and six stools. The unfortunate James II could hardly have laid his head on the pillow of his magnificent new bed, for by December of that year he had fled his kingdom.

An eagle-eyed detective with privileged access to the Knole furnishings can find the evidence of Lord Dorset's trawl. The walnut armchairs and stools covered in red silk damask in the Spangle Bedroom are stamped underneath with WP for Whitehall Palace and a crown. On closer inspection the brass locks in the Cartoon Gallery reveal William III's monogram. Even the close stool – the seventeenth-century lavatory – in the King's Closet was probably used by the Stuart kings.

Dorset resigned as Lord Chamberlain in 1697, and after all the promise and glories of his early years, the final part of his life was far from happy. According to his grandson, he was 'Extenuated by Pleasure and Indulgences and sinking under premature Old Age'. In 1706 his marriage to his former housekeeper Anne Roche, 'of very obscure Connexions', so concerned his family that they considered having him put under some form of restraint. Matthew Prior, dispatched to report on his state of mind, wrote sadly, 'He drivels so much better Sense even now than any other Man can talk, that you must not call me into Court as a Witness.' In fact this proved unnecessary, for Charles Sackville, 6th Earl of Dorset, died later that year. The great collection of furniture at Knole is the lasting legacy of this extraordinary man, described in an epitaph by Alexander Pope as 'the grace of Courts, the Muses' pride'.

Dressing up

'This morning went to see Mr Wade at Snowshill to talk about the old carriages he offered the Trust. Also persuaded him to leave us his fine collection of clothes which he had suggested bequeathing to some museum.' So recorded James Lees-Milne, the National Trust's Historic Buildings Secretary, in his diary on 6 August 1948. Charles Paget Wade had been negotiating with the National Trust for some fifteen years about the transfer of his house, Snowshill Manor in Gloucestershire, and its contents.

House and contents in this context meant a collection of collections, for Wade was an inveterate gatherer, having started at the age of seven. Following in the tradition of William Morris and the Arts and Crafts Movement, he believed passionately in the importance of conserving things that had been produced by man's hands rather than by machine. With a fortune inherited from sugar plantations in the West Indies, and a charming, dilapidated Cotswold manor house purchased after seeing an advertisement in *Country Life* while fighting in the First World War, Wade was able both to collect and to house his collection to his heart's content. At Snowshill today, the visitor can marvel at collections of bicycles, kitchen bygones, oriental lacquer cabinets, and even Japanese Samurai armour.

But one of Wade's most important collections, the costume collection referred to by James Lees-Milne, cannot be seen there. This was built up by Wade partly because he was fascinated by the craftmanship required in both the manufacture of textiles and the making of clothes before the coming of industrial techniques, and partly because he loved dressing up. Indeed, James Lees-Milne considered Wade the

Charles Paget Wade on the steps of Snowshill Manor, wearing a set of Cromwellian armour from his costume collection. (NT)

Paulise de Bush photographed in 1905 with her grandmother. (NTPL/John Hammond)

most eccentric of all the donors to the National Trust that he had met – no mean feat in a contest replete with eccentric contenders – describing how Wade wore his hair 'square-cut, shoulder length' in the Roundhead style, and dressed in a trunk and hose. When he entertained friends like John Betjeman and Clough Williams Ellis, he provided them with authentic eighteenth- and nineteenth-century costumes for their charades.

The clothes bequeathed to the Trust consisted of over 2,000 items of male and female dress including countryman's smocks, servants' livery, military uniforms and religious habits. But the superb heart of the collection are the fine eighteenth-century court costumes. By the middle of that century, English gentlemen and their families wore clothes of practical materials and styles for their life in the country, but for attendance at court would don the satins and silks that had been everyday attire for their aristocratic predecessors. Wade acquired examples of the *robe à la française* or sackback dress, a style perfected by Madame du Pompadour, mistress of Louis XV and queen of French fashion. Derived from a loose negligée, worn in the privacy of the home, it developed into a loose dress worn over a tight bodice, with a full petticoat. At the back the train fell in pleats from the neckline to the floor, allowing an expensive and beautiful material to be fully displayed.

Gentlemen attending levées at the Court of St James would not be overshadowed by this magnificence. The Snowshill collection contains elaborate court coats and waistcoats, their surface covered in rich embellishment that included light-catching elements such as glass, foil and spangles so that they might glitter in the candlelight. The diarist Mrs Delany criticised Lord Villiers for his costume at a court event in 1773, 'pale purple velvet coat, turned up with lemon-colour, and embroidered all over with S.S's of pearl as big as pease, and in all the spaces little medallions in beaten gold, *real solid*, in various figures of *Cupids*.' But for two examples collected by Wade that show an equal richness, we might have accused Mrs Delany of exaggeration. They are remarkable survivals, for often court costumes were dismantled once they were out of fashion, and their gold and silver wire and threads sold back to the laceman.

Because of the fragility of the Snowshill costumes, they are kept in store at Berrington Hall in Herefordshire. Students of costume history can apply to see them (see p.2), but some of the finest examples have been photographed and reproduced in *The Art of Dress* published by the National Trust.

The Trust does, however, have a large costume collection regularly on public display at Killerton House in Devon. The core of this collection was created by Paulise de Bush. Her background had Ruritanian overtones, for her father travelled in Europe as an 'ambassador' for his family's firm of manufacturing chemists, and was created a Baron of the Duchy of Saxe-Coburg and Gotha. Her mother was a celebrated American opera singer. Born in 1900, Paulise inherited her father's title when she was three years old. She became fascinated by the theatre, and married the director Herbert Lugg in 1933. Together they staged Shakespearean plays in their Berkshire home, collecting period and theatrical costumes. Some of the early costumes were salvaged from an old house in the same Berkshire village, where they had been locked away and forgotten by former occupants. Paulise, recognising they were too precious for theatricals, began her own historical collection, augmenting it with purchases from Christie's and Sotheby's.

When Paulise died in 1975 she left about 700 costumes to the National Trust: these came to the Acland family home at Killerton, under the curatorship of Atherton Harrison, the stage costume designer. In addition to clothing for men, women and children from the mid-seventeenth century to the present day, fashion plates, haberdashery items, underwear and *cartes de visite* have been collected to show how fashion was disseminated and garments were made. Among the most spectacular exhibits is a late Victorian corset on a stand emblazoned with the combined flags of Great Britain and France which would have stood under a glass dome on a shop counter.

The collection, added to over the years, now contains more than 9,000 articles. Each year a selection of articles is put on display in a themed exhibition. In 1999 the exhibition will examine major themes in twentieth-century dress.

A Passion for Plants

The strange and wonderful garden at Biddulph Grange in Staffordshire was created from 1840 by James and Maria Bateman. Horticultural fashion had moved on from the natural landscapes of Capability Brown, of expanses of grass and water with plantations of mainly native trees. Early in the century Humphry Repton had advocated that the garden near a house should use flowering shrubs and trees that were now coming into Britain from all over the world. This theme was developed by John Claudius Loudon, who considered plants to be the most important element of a garden, whether in shrubberies, flower beds or conservatories. So great was his passion for collecting plants that in the garden attached to his London house, which covered less than quarter of an acre, he grew more than 2,000 species.

James Bateman acquired the plant-collecting passion at the age of eight: 'I was devoted to orchids long before I knew what an orchid was, indeed the word itself was quite strange to me when I heard my mother apply it to a beautiful plant with spotted leaves and speckled flowers which I had gathered in a country lane and regarded with great admiration.' As a wealthy undergraduate at Oxford in 1833 he was able to send a plant-collector, Thomas Colley, to British Guiana to search for orchids, and four years later he established his international reputation by publishing *Orchidaceae of Mexico and Guatemala*, the largest botanical book ever produced.

In 1838 James Bateman married Maria Egerton-Warburton. Theirs was a true gardening marriage, for she too was an enthusiastic horticulturist with a particular passion for herbaceous plants such as fuchsias, roses and lilies. Two years after their marriage, the Batemans set up home at Biddulph Grange, extending the existing vicarage in an Italian style and adding a series of conservatories to house their collections of rhododendrons, camellias, ferns and orchids.

They also began to lay out the grounds, beginning with the formal gardens near the house. Taking advantage of the sloping terrain, they created a series of parterres, each with a different feature, so that one had roses, another Monkey Puzzle trees, another verbenas. This idea of theming was continued throughout the grounds to create a 'world image' garden, with an Italian formal garden near the house, a Rhododendron Ground, the Glen, where ferns and rhododendrons could flourish in a moist and shady microclimate, China, a spectacular recreation of a scene from a willow-pattern plate, and Egypt where yew was trained and clipped to resemble a

A Victorian orchid collector at work. (The Lindley Library)

temple with obelisks. This world image garden in some ways echoed the great trade exhibitions of the period. Just as these celebrated the world's manufacturing achievements, so Biddulph became a celebration of horticultural achievements combined with discoveries of plants from distant lands.

Many of the plants for Biddulph came from Loddiges' Nursery in Hackney, East London, established in the 1770s by Conrad Loddige, a German émigré from Hanover. Over the years the nursery expanded, so that by the 1820s, when it was under the management of Conrad's sons, William and George, it had the greatest plant collection in the world, overtaking even that held at the Royal Botanic Gardens at Kew.

The Loddiges used a worldwide network of correspondents to provide them with plants and seeds. Some of these were amateur enthusiasts, such as missionaries and government officers. Others were professional plant-hunters, often backed by institutions like the Horticultural Society and wealthy investors like James Bateman. Joseph Hooker, who was to succeed his father Sir William as Director at Kew, brought back exotic rhododendrons from Sikkim, some of which were given to the Batemans and planted in the Glen.

Perhaps the most famous and intrepid of the plant-hunters was David Douglas. As a result of his travels in North America in the 1820s he introduced many new plants, including *Pseudotsuga menziesii*, the Douglas fir. His diary of his South American trip, which lasted for two years, vividly shows the life endured by plant-collectors in search of their prey: 'travelled 33 miles, drenched and bleached with rain and sleet, chilled with a piercing north wind; and then to finish the day experienced the cooling comfortless consolation of lying down wet without supper or fire. On such occasions I am very liable to become fretful.' It was a dangerous life, too: Douglas was to end his life by falling into a pit in Honolulu where he was gored by a wild bull.

Another important plant hunter was Robert Fortune, the Horticultural Society's collector in China. Taking advantage of the Treaty of Nanking, signed in 1842 at the end of the Opium War, he travelled to areas previously closed to Europeans. Even then, he often had to disguise himself as a Chinaman, as on a visit to Suchow, where he triumphantly recorded the discovery of 'a white Glycine [wisteria], a fine new double yellow rose, and a gardenia with white blossoms like a camellia. These plants are now in England and will soon be met with in every garden in the country.'

Plants collected by Douglas and Fortune were transported to Britain in Wardian cases. The invention of Dr Nathaniel Ward in 1833, these were in essence portable miniature greenhouses, enabling live plants to be shipped long distances. The new plants could then be successfully propagated by Loddiges and other nurserymen for patrons like Bateman.

After the careful stewardship of the Batemans, Biddulph suffered dramatic vicissitudes in fortune. By the 1980s the garden had fallen into such disrepair that the National Trust undertook a major restoration programme. Nevertheless, a few plants brought to England by Robert Fortune do survive. In the Chinese Garden, for instance, *Pseudolarix amabilis*, probably introduced from China in 1852, is still there. A second example had blown down, but examination of its rings showed their age. The Trust, meanwhile, has replanted many examples of plants first brought in by the Victorian plant-hunters. Thus visitors to the Glen and the Rhododendron Ground can see again the exotic species collected by Sir Joseph Hooker in Nepal in the 1850s, and admire in the Bowling Green *Pinus ponderosa*, the Western yellow pine introduced to Britain from North America by David Douglas in 1826.

William John Bankes, from a study made by Sir George Hayter in 1836. (NTPL/Angelo Hornak)

Egyptian stela, *or tomb inscription from the workmen's village at Deir el-Medina, just outside Thebes in Upper Egypt. This is one of twenty-five* stelae *collected by William Bankes. (NTPL/Derrick E. Witty)*

The Curiosity of the Traveller

William John Bankes was a man blessed with wealth, privilege, looks, charm and intelligence. He was born in 1786, the second son of Henry Bankes of Kingston Hall in Dorset, and the noted beauty Frances Woodley. Already set to inherit from his great-uncle, William Wynne, he became heir to the enormous Bankes estates in 1806 when his brother Henry was drowned in a shipping accident. At Trinity College Cambridge he befriended Lord Byron, who dubbed him 'my collegiate pastor and master and patron' who 'ruled the Roast or rather the Roasting – and was father of all our Mischiefs'. In 1812 he was one of the leading lights of the London season, losing his heart to the bluestocking Anabel Milbanke. She rejected his suit, and that of Byron, though she was to change her mind about the latter after the success of *Childe Harolde*.

In that same year William Wynne wrote to his great-nephew, 'all the world is now open to the curiosity of the Traveller'. Taking these words firmly to heart, he set off for Spain to spend two years acquiring paintings amid the disruptions of the Peninsular War. Some of the works that he bought at this time are still at Kingston Lacy, including a fragment of a putto. He wrote to his bemused father that a French soldier had cut it out of Murillo's great masterpiece, the *Jubileo della Porciuncula*, then in the Capuchin convent in Seville, to use as the cover for his knapsack. In fact the *Jubileo* is complete and now in Cologne.

In December 1814 Bankes sailed from Spain to embark on his Middle Eastern travels. He took as his guide Giovanni Finati, and later wrote down and published his *Life and Adventures*, a detailed account of their journeying through Syria and Egypt. These were exciting times, and Bankes took full advantage, making the dangerous journey across the desert to Zenobia's ancient capital at Palmyra, visiting the famous Middle Eastern traveller, Lady Hester Stanhope, and penetrating Petra dressed as a Bedouin, one of the first Europeans to do so.

For his travels up the Nile, Bankes gathered together a talented group that included three artists, the faithful Finati, and Giovanni Belzoni, formerly the Patagonian Samson who had fascinated audiences at Sadler's Wells with his feats of strength. Now he was a hydraulic engineer and pioneer archaeologist, a combination that proved invaluable when Bankes decided to ship the obelisk of Philae back to Dorset. The venture started badly when the monument nearly sank to the bottom of the Nile, but it eventually made it to Kingston, where its foundations were laid in the grounds in 1827 by the Duke of Wellington.

But Bankes was not just a treasure hunter. His recording and publication of the Greek and hieroglyphic inscriptions on the obelisk proved an important step towards unravelling the mystery of ancient Egyptian language. His group copied wall paintings in rock tombs at Beni Hasan, excavated at El-Sebua in Nubia and at Abydos, and spent a month at Abu Simbel working on the great temple of Ramses II that Johann Burckhardt had rescued from the invading sands a few years earlier. Working up ladders by candlelight in the stifling heat, Bankes and his companions copied the wonderful, vibrant wall paintings within the temple. These drawings are now part of the Egyptian collection in the former housekeeper's room at Kingston Lacy. Ignoring Burckhardt's warning 'not to bury your treasures at your country house, where they can never generally be admired', Bankes gathered small antiquities, twenty-five tomb inscriptions from the workmen's village of Deir el-Medina and fragments of tomb paintings from the necropolis at Thebes.

From Egypt Bankes moved on to Venice, where he joined his Cambridge friend, Lord Byron, and added more paintings to his collection. He bought two particularly fine pictures at this time: Sebastiano del Piombo's *Judgement of Solomon* painted in the early sixteenth century, and Velasquez's portrait of Cardinal Camillo Massimi, painted in 1649–50. But the 'great traveller', as he was described by Mrs Arbuthnot, had journeyed enough for the moment, and returning to England in 1820, he devoted the next twenty years to his family inheritance. He began to pester his father to remodel Kingston Hall. He greatly admired the work of Inigo Jones and was under the impression that he had designed Kingston: in fact the house was built by the Restoration architect Roger Pratt in the 1660s, but had been considerably altered over the years. Henry Bankes resisted all blandishments, but died in 1834, and William was master of the estate. He commissioned Charles Barry, whom he had met in Egypt, to restore the house to its seventeenth-century appearance and to make it a more comfortable home.

However, William's plans were thrown into disarray in September 1841 when he was accused of indecently exposing himself with a soldier of the Foot Guards in London's Green Park. He had been caught in a similar situation some eight years earlier, but the Duke of Wellington had stepped in to protect him. This time the Iron Duke could do nothing so, unlike Oscar Wilde, Bankes decided that discretion was the better part of valour and, jumping bail, fled to Italy. From his exile in Venice he continued to commission works of art and furnishings for his house, now known as Kingston Lacy. Although his brother George handled his business affairs for him, William distrusted his taste, so it was his sister, Lady Falmouth, who carried out his instructions on the refurbishment. So detailed were these schemes that he even sent notes about the amount of gilding to be applied.

This vicarious collecting is well exemplified by the Spanish Room, the former dining room which he turned into a gallery for his paintings. From seventeenth-century Venetian palaces came an ornate baroque ceiling and tooled and painted leather wall hangings. The three pairs of doors contained twelve pear wood panels decorated with motifs of the months painted by a Venetian artist assisted by Bankes himself.

Legends have persisted that during his years of exile, he visited the house clandestinely, taking advantage of the fact that the family estate reached down to the Dorset coast. Recently evidence has come to light to show that legend was indeed truth and that William John Bankes visited Kingston several times in 1854, knowing he was mortally ill. At last he could see in reality the schemes that had only existed in his very original imagination.

Good Husbandry

Elizabeth Talbot, Dowager Countess of Shrewsbury, known to posterity as Bess of Hardwick, died on 13 February 1608 the richest woman in England. In her will she listed her various houses, their lavish contents and furnishings, and her personal possessions. All this magnificence and wealth would have astonished those present at Bess's birth some eighty years earlier. She was born at Hardwick in Derbyshire in 1527, one of a family of four girls and one boy. Her father was a member of the minor gentry, owning a few hundred acres and a small manor house. When he died the following year, he could leave each of his daughters only the very slight sum of £26 13s 4d.

From these modest beginnings, Bess built up her personal fortune through her four marriages, the last to the Earl of Shrewsbury, premier peer of the realm, and by her astute and careful husbandry. This is not to say that she was miserly: in a telling rebuke to her steward at Chatsworth concerning the treatment of her half-sister, Jane Leche, she wrote, 'I cannot like it to have my sister so used. Like as I would not have any superfluity or waste of anything, so likewise would I have her to have that which is needful and necessary.'

Though many of Bess's houses have vanished or, in the case of Chatsworth, altered beyond recognition, the Old and New Halls at Hardwick give an idea of her style of living. She acquired the Old Hall, her birthplace, from her bankrupt brother in 1583 and began to enlarge it. When her last husband, Lord Shrewsbury, died in 1590, she stopped work and with the money now at her disposal began at once to build a completely new and very grand house – the New Hall – just a few yards from the existing house. Old Hall is now a ruin, but the New Hall, for many years the dower house in the shadow of Chatsworth, is a remarkable survival. So too is the great collection of late sixteenth- and early seventeenth-century textiles and furnishings it contains. Many of these textiles were acquired by Bess herself; indeed many were worked in her household under her direct supervision.

In her account of the collection, *An Elizabethan Inheritance*, Santina Levey explains the importance of these textiles as 'the major means of providing colour, pattern, warmth and comfort within a house'. Perhaps the most important survivals are two sets of large wall hangings now mounted behind glass in the Entrance Hall and on the Chapel Landing at Hardwick. The first set depicts famous women of the Ancient World, each flanked by personifications of her virtues. Thus Penelope is shown with Patience and Perseverance; Lucretia with Chastity and Liberality. The second set illustrates the three Virtues with their opposite vices personified, so Faith is shown with Mahomet, Hope with Judas (a fragment, not on display), and Temperance with Sardanapalus, who symbolises over-indulgence. Bess may have replaced the more usual Charity by Temperance because she felt strongly about this virtue, remembering her father's improvidence. Indeed, her second daughter was named Temperance. Bess herself identified with the faithful wife, Penelope, and named her last child Lucretia, so these hangings have strong personal links.

They are of applied work, using velvets and silks, some of which came from church vestments. They were made in the 1570s at Chatsworth by a professional embroiderer, Thomas Lane, and we know a lot about them because they became a bone of contention between Bess and Lord Shrewsbury in the quarrels that finally broke up their marriage. Shrewsbury had tried to claim that they were part of his estate but Bess was able to prove that the materials had come from ecclesiastical copes acquired by her second and third husbands, William Cavendish and William St Loe, following the dispersal of monastic possessions.

Bess herself was an accomplished needlewoman, and she and her family and upper servants would have worked on some of the smaller pieces of embroidery. The larger pieces, however, would have been created for her by professional embroiderers like Lane, and the accounts for Hardwick refer to nine pairs of beams, used as adjustable embroidery frames, set up in the New Hall. Here they would have worked at pieces such as the appliqué embroidery panel in red velvet decorated with silver strapwork, now in the Exhibition Room at Hardwick. In the centre of this piece are the initials ES for Elizabeth Shrewsbury.

Elizabeth Talbot, Countess of Shrewsbury: a portrait painted in the 1590s when she was building the New Hall at Hardwick. (NT)

For warmth and comfort, Bess purchased tapestries and Turkey carpets: her accounts show that in the two Halls at Hardwick she had forty-eight sets of tapestry and thirty-eight carpets. Three sets of tapestry came from the bankrupt estates of Sir Christopher Hatton, one of Elizabeth I's leading courtiers and admirers, who ruined himself building his great house of Holdenby in Northamptonshire. From his nephew, Bess acquired the thirteen tapestries illustrating Gideon's Triumph in 1592. She paid £326 15s 9d for them, but had the bill reduced because she had to replace the Hatton coat of arms with her own. Being canny, she merely covered the existing arms with painted canvas. The Gideon tapestries are exceptionally large, too deep to be hung over panelling. But Bess bought them while she was still planning Hardwick, so the scale of the hangings dictated the dimensions of the Long Gallery, where they are still to be seen today.

Carpets were very luxurious items in the sixteenth century, used principally for display on tables and cupboards, although the Hardwick inventory of 1601 records that seven were floor coverings. This inventory is careful to distinguish between Turkey work, oriental carpets from Persia and India brought to England by Turkey merchants, and English Turkey work, a pile wool fabric knotted in the Turkish manner on a warp of linen or hemp. One fine example of the latter is a table carpet now on display in the Paved Room, showing *The Judgement of Paris*, framed by the Hardwick stags and Bess's arms and dated 1574.

Just as her initials, Countess's coronet and heraldic stags proclaim Bess's wealth and position from the skyline of Hardwick, so her textiles and embroideries proved her status. Not only did they feature in her quarrels with her husband, they also are an important part of her will, written in April 1601. In this she instructs her heirs to 'have special care and regard, and to preserve the same from all manner of wet, moth, and other hurte and spoil thereof'. And indeed, that is precisely what her descendants have done.

Spoils of War

Powis Castle in Powys is full of surprises. It was built by the Welsh princes of Powys some time around 1200, taking full advantage of the defensive nature of the site, a great limestone outcrop. Although it still looks like a medieval stronghold, the interior is a comfortable country house, while the rising ground was used to produce one of Britain's most spectacular terraced gardens. A former curtain wall converted into a ballroom range now houses one of the most important collections of Indian artefacts in Europe, the Clive Museum.

The collection was gathered together by two generations of Clives: Robert Clive, the great administrator known to posterity as 'Clive of India', and his eldest son, Edward, 2nd Lord Clive, who in 1784 married Henrietta Herbert, daughter of Lord Powis.

Robert Clive went out to India in 1744 as a young Writer or Cadet of the East India Company. England's military conflict with France over the matter of the Austrian Succession in Europe inevitably spilt over to India and Clive transferred to the Company's army. Raising the siege of Arcot in 1752 he earned the title of Sabit Jang, Steady in War, and his military reputation grew as he won a series of victories over the French. His finest hour came in 1757 with the Battle of Plassey where he defeated Siraj-ad-daula, Nawab of Bengal, enabling Mir Jafar to take the throne. A grateful Mir Jafar gave Britain £3 million, of which Clive's share came to over £200,000. At the age of thirty-two he was virtually dictator of Bengal, and a hero in English eyes.

During his sojourns in India, Clive began to acquire Indian artefacts. The majority of the articles that he accumulated were either spoils of war or gifts presented to him by Indian princes. A significant group represent indigenous Indian traditions, in particular the cult centred on Vishnu. A second group reflect the lifestyle of Indian Mughal nobility of the mid-eighteenth century, and include artefacts such as huqqas for smoking tobacco, rosewater sprinklers and pan boxes, which contained chopped areca nuts and aromatic spices taken as a *digestif*. When Clive returned to England in 1767 he sent in advance 'A chest full of shawls, Pictures, Swords and other Curiosities'.

At this time Robert Clive's fame was at its height. He was reckoned to be worth the colossal sum of £401,102. But Nemesis was approaching: his deteriorating health led him to take increasing amounts of opium and, moreover, his enemies were gathering. Horace Walpole had long taken exception to Clive's great wealth; grumbling about rising prices in 1762 he had sneered, 'I expect a pint of milk will not be sold under a diamond, and then nobody can keep a cow but my Lord Clive.' A parliamentary motion to impeach Clive for corruption was defeated in May 1773, and Edmund Burke declared 'Lord Clive has thus come out of the fiery trial much brighter than when he went into it. . . . His reputation too, for ability, stands higher than ever.' But within eighteen months Clive of India was dead, his old enemy Walpole writing 'Lord Clive has died every death in the parish register; at present it is fashionable to believe he cut his throat.'

Robert Clive's Indian collection was inherited by his eldest son Edward, who also

Tipu on his Golden Throne, by a South Indian artist, c.1800. (Courtesy of the Earl of Powis and the Powis Estate Trustees)

made his career in India. In 1798 he went out with his wife Henrietta and daughters to become Governor of Madras, responsible for the administration of Southern India. The region had been in a state of foment since 1758 when a Muslim adventurer, Haidar Ali, began attacking the British. Although in 1792 Haidar's son Tipu Sahib had been forced to accept a humiliating peace treaty at the hands of Lord Cornwallis, Tipu's hatred for the British remained. A man obsessed by tigers, he had a wooden carving made of a tiger mauling a European, and inside installed a miniature organ with keyboard and bellows to simulate the man's cries. This sinister object is now in London's Victoria and Albert Museum.

Tipu has become very much the villain of British history in India. He was, in fact, an able ruler, very learned with a fine library. But his hatred of the British drove him to open negotiations with Napoleon which was more than the Governor General, Lord Mornington, could stomach. He mobilised an army, and Tipu's capital, Seringapatam, was stormed on 4 May 1799. Tipu fell in the assault, and South India's richest city was laid open to looting by the British. Mornington's brother Arthur Wellesley, later Duke of Wellington, was a horrified witness:

> Scarcely a house in the town was left unplundered, and I understand that in camp jewels of the greatest value, bars of gold, etc, etc, have been offered for sale in the bazaars of the army by our soldiers, sepoys, and followers. I came in

> to take the command on the morning of the 5th, and by the greatest exertion, by hanging, flogging, etc, in the course of that day, I restored order.

The plunder was duly divided up and some of Tipu's personal possessions were given to Lord and Lady Clive: a jewelled tiger's head from the rail of his throne; a beautiful tent of printed and painted cotton, decorated with roses; and a pair of filigree and enamel rosewater sprinklers, thought to have come from his bedroom.

Lord Clive stayed on in India until 1803. Soon after he returned to England his brother-in-law, Lord Powis, died unmarried, and Clive inherited the title and estate of Powis Castle. The collection of Indian artefacts gathered over two generations was installed in the former ballroom of the castle along with Lady Clive's botanical and geological collections, and a fully stocked menagerie that included Tipu's mare, Sultana.

Robert and Edward Clive were not the only collectors of Indian art and artefacts, but their collection is now very important because it has survived remarkably intact. It has been reinstalled in the ballroom and the visitor today can be as astonished as the Rev. Evans who, in 1809, was startled to come upon 'the model of an elephant, covered with a coat of mail [now on show in the Royal Armouries in Leeds], with two Indians upon its back brought from India by the late Lord Clive.'

Natural Collectors

For the Harpur Crewes of Calke Abbey in Derbyshire, collecting became a family trait. The baroque house, built by Sir John Harpur in the opening years of the eighteenth century, gradually filled with contents gathered by generations of the family, so that when Henry Harpur-Crewe handed Calke over to the National Trust in 1985, it was bursting at the seams. Some individual treasures came to light, such as a Shudi harpsichord found in the stable loft, and, most spectacularly, an early eighteenth-century state bed, still in its original packing cases, discovered in the housekeeper's bedroom. A significant proportion of the contents, however, were collections – horse paintings, dolls and toys, carriages, and above all natural history.

Much has been made of the eccentricity of the Harpur Crewes – and indeed some members of the family were very extraordinary. But in one respect they showed a remarkable consistency, they were fascinated by the natural world. This interest apparently dates back to Sir Henry Harpur, the 7th baronet who was known as the 'isolated baronet' because in 1792 he married a lady's maid, Nanette Hawkins, and withdrew from society. One of his favourite occupations was to watch wild animals in the park at Calke. He also began the collection of taxidermy, an interest inherited by his grandson, Sir John Harpur Crewe, so that by 1840 there were 400 cases of birds, quadrupeds and fish in the house.

Sir John extended his collecting to geological, fossil and conchological specimens. Many of these, carefully assembled, are now on show in the Saloon, but other cases scattered through the house are more random, with shells and snails muddled up with fossil fish and beach detritus.

Sir John's fascination for natural history was echoed by his wife's interest in plant collecting and cultivation. Georgina, Lady Crewe reorganised the flower garden at Calke, installing the auricula theatre in one corner. This structure, the only one of its kind to survive, has tiered shelving so that auriculas, and other potted plants could be displayed through the seasons. She shared her horticultural interests with her husband's cousin, the Rev. Henry Harpur Crewe, rector of Drayton Beauchamp in Buckinghamshire. In the 1820s, fifty-eight varieties of ephemeral hybrid geraniums were growing at Calke, including 'Calkensis' and 'Crewensis', and the Reverend rescued from extinction *Cheiranthus* 'Harpur Crewe' a small yellow wallflower now widely grown.

Passion for natural history, along with the family's tendency to reclusiveness and eccentricity, reached its apogee with Sir John's son, Vauncey Harpur Crewe, the 10th baronet, who inherited Calke in 1886. His collections included 10,000 specimens of British butterflies and moths, 1,500 birds' eggs and several thousand specimens of higher plants, mosses, lichens and fungi. What remains at Calke represents probably less than half the original, as many lepidoptera, some stuffed birds and eggs – including the celebrated Great Auk's egg bought for 300 guineas in 1894 – were sold to meet taxes following Sir Vauncey's death in 1924. Pests too have taken their toll. However, in the substantial collection that remains, there are many rarities.

Sir Vauncey was also a keen taxidermist, going on shooting expeditions with his exotically named gamekeeper, Agathos Pegg. Together they would prepare carcasses for stuffing. One of the most poignant sights that met National Trust staff when they undertook the inventory of contents of Calke in 1985 was the small skins hanging in the bedrooms, still awaiting treatment from Sir Vauncey.

He also bought taxidermy from dealers, who would produce diorama cases for him. Thomas Gunn of Norwich, and his son Frederick for example, produced cases of Bewick's and whooper swans, capercaillie and great bustards. In the Saloon there are several good displays of mammals: four adult foxes with cubs, four otters, badgers, red squirrels, stoats and weasels. Sir Vauncey was also fascinated by hybrids, freaks and colour varieties. Among these bizarre exhibits are white and partly white blackbirds, all-white lapwings, robins, house martins and jackdaws. Frederick Gunn produced a series of watercolours for him, showing birds in freak plumage. When part of the collection was put up for sale, the catalogue alluded to 'unique and remarkable varieties ... albinos, melanistic, pied ... also a large number of hybrids, chiefly of game birds'.

When Sir Vauncey died in 1924, the photograph distributed to his tenants showed him in country clothes, with his gun over his shoulder. This was a characteristic pose, he was never parted from his gun except on Sundays when he left it in the church porch while attending morning service. But he was no ordinary shooting squire: his bag was for ornithology, not the pot. The park at Calke was in effect a private wildlife sanctuary, while in the estate beyond, agricultural tenants were forbidden to trim hedges so that cover might be provided for nesting birds.

Calke Park is centred on a wooded valley with a stream dammed to produce a chain of ponds. Its landscape is rich and varied, with gnarled oaks and bracken,

Sir Vauncey Harpur Crewe in a typical pose, with a gun over his shoulder. This photograph was distributed to his tenants on his death in 1924. (NT)

grassland, and strategically placed specimen trees. The oaks and bracken are the last remnants of medieval woodland in the area, and it is thought that the Bainbridges, who purchased Calke in 1585, deliberately bought up these remnants to preserve them at a time of concentrated felling and clearing for construction of houses and ships. When the Harpurs took over, they used the park for deer, undertaking a certain amount of landscaping, and added some land. Then came the 'isolated baronet', who instructed his servants to allow hares and pheasants to breed within sight of his windows, undisturbed by keepers, dogs and cats. The park became a private place, particularly in Sir Vauncey's time when motor cars were banned and any visitors that did get to Calke were required to walk or use horses and carriages.

The result of this reclusiveness is that Calke is one of the best parks in Britain for insects, mainly beetles. A survey recently recorded 250 species in the old trees, bracken glades and around the ponds. These medieval woods are the relict of Derbyshire forest cover dating back to 5000 BC, so that the species protected by Sir Vauncey and his predecessors and still surviving in the park are direct descendants of the original 'wildwood fauna'.

A Determined Collector

In 1949 the National Trust acquired Arlington Court on the death of Rosalie Chichester. She bequeathed her family home, a Greek Revival villa dating from the early nineteenth century, together with its estate of 3,500 acres in North Devon. She also left the Trust her collections. As the guidebook puts it:

> Her collector's instinct had developed into a mania. ...she had amassed 75 cabinets full of shells, 200 model ships, several hundred pieces of pewter, 50 punch ladles, 30 tea caddies, two cases full of candle snuffers, two cases of Maori skirts and African clubs, five large cases of stuffed birds, hundreds of snuff boxes, a large stamp collection with some 52,000 specimens, 30 volumes of Xmas and greetings cards ...

And so the list goes on. Seemingly every aspect of Miss Chichester's life impelled her to collect – the Trust even found a case of bombs and Zeppelin bits – and some of this disparate collection had to be sold simply to enable visitors to move around the house. On the estate, meanwhile, there was yet another collection – of wildlife – inspired by Rosalie Chichester's visits to Australia and New Zealand. A small flock of Jacob sheep and a herd of Shetland ponies, offspring of the animals first established here, still roam happily in the park.

Rosalie Caroline was born in 1865, the only child of Sir Bruce and Rosalie Chichester. Her father's passion was yacht racing, an interest he shared with her maternal grandfather, Thomas Chamberlayne, whose cutter *Arrow* was the only British yacht to defeat the schooner *America*, after which the America's Cup is named. When Rosalie was three years old she was taken on the first of two Mediterranean cruises by her father on his schooner *Erminia*. The experience inspired her both to travel the world, and to acquire numerous model ships – one of the many collections at Arlington.

The ship collection now consists of about eighty models, exhibited in various rooms of the house. Many of the early nineteenth-century examples were made by French prisoners during the Napoleonic Wars. The long hours of confinement were whiled away by making exquisite frigates, sloops, and two- and three-decker warships from animal bones or pieces of wood, with silk or hair for the riggings. In the Ship Lobby is a large-scale model of *HMS Louisa*, a two-decker fifth rate lost in a violent storm off Holland in 1736. The model was probably made to hang in church as a memorial to the ship's crew.

Rosalie Chichester augmented these with a selection of the varied craft employed at the evacuation of Dunkirk. Between 26 May and 3 June 1940, under 'Operation Dynamo', over 1,300 vessels helped to rescue 300,000 British and French soldiers trapped on the beaches of Dunkirk. The collection includes tugs, coasters, a motor picket boat used to pick up men to transport them to the larger vessels waiting off shore, and an 'R' class destroyer.

The latest addition to the collection, however, was made by the National Trust: a silver model of *Gypsy Moth IV*, the yacht in which Sir Francis Chichester, Rosalie's step-nephew, made his epic round-the-world voyage in 1966–7. Yachting was in the family's blood, but it brought tragedy to the young Rosalie, for her father contracted Maltese fever during one of their cruises on *Erminia* and died in 1881 leaving his estate heavily mortgaged. Two years later Lady Chichester married Sir Arthur Chichester, a distant cousin, so Rosalie took up the weighty task of running the Arlington estate and bringing it back to financial health. She spent the rest of her life doing this with the help of her companion Chrissie Peters. In 1921, and again in 1928, Miss Chichester and Miss Peters went on world tours, adding exotic items such as the Maori skirts and African clubs to the Arlington collections.

Rosalie Chichester may have liked exotica, but one of her most important collections is very domestic: the pewter collection. In the sixteenth and seventeenth centuries, before the widespread use of glass and pottery, pewter was used for table-

Rosalie Chichester (3rd from right) with her companion, Chrissie Peters (4th from right), on tour in New Zealand in 1928. (NTPL/John Hammond)

ware – cups, plates, bowls and candlesticks. When brightly polished, pewter resembles silver but is also soft, so that even a moderately hard cut from a knife will damage the surface. Thus, while much pewter tableware was made, it needed constant burnishing and was often melted down and re-used. The Elizabethan porringer, a small dish decorated with clover-leafed ears, in the Arlington collection is therefore a comparative rarity, as are four Stuart candlesticks. Several pewter spoons are decorated with a cast portrait of Queen Anne. These are early examples of souvenirs made specially for a coronation: in this case in 1702.

Scottish pewterware is represented by long sets of ale and spirit measures used by tavern keepers. A set of thistle-shaped measures dating from the mid-nineteenth century are particularly unusual because soon after they were issued, it was discovered that they did not drain fully, and should have been destroyed. This rare set escaped.

Chrissie Peters died in 1939, and Rosalie Chichester's last years were rather lonely, as she coped with the restrictions of the Second World War and increasing ill-health. One visitor who came to Arlington at this time paints a touching picture:

> The morning room was smallish and darkish and crammed with furniture – footstools, what-nots, *guéridons*, easels, cabinets full of knicknacks. There was

> an impression of thick plush curtains and velvet upholstery, of fringes and screens. Enthroned amongst the clutter, in a black shapeless garment, was Miss Chichester, mosque-shaped, enormous.

This clutter has perforce had to be removed, but two cabinets in the Lobby reflect some of Rosalie Chichester's style. They were arranged by Jan Newman, house parlourman from 1927 until his retirement in 1974, and one of the people who helped the Trust to reorganise the house after Miss Chichester's death. Here are her fans, parasols, jewellery, together with Primrose League badges, a silver plaque awarded to her by *The Practical Photographer*, and a silver medal won in the 'Womanhood Competition'. A fitting tribute to a remarkable woman.

A Very Expensive Library

When Sir Henry Hobart, a rich lawyer, built himself a fine new mansion at Blickling in Norfolk in 1619, a library would not have been included in his plans. Sir Henry may have owned books, but these would have been kept in chests in his closet near his bedchamber. Country-house libraries designed specifically to accommodate books made their appearance in England only after the Restoration in 1660.

Blickling does, however, have one of the finest country-house collections of books in Britain, inherited by Sir Henry's great-great-grandson, the 1st Earl of Buckinghamshire, in 1745. It came from a distant kinsman, Sir Richard Ellys of Nocton in Lincolnshire. Horace Walpole described Sir Richard as 'a rich, childless baronet ...[who] pretended to learning on the credit of a very expensive library'. But Walpole was not entirely correct in this characteristically sharp assessment, for Ellys's taste in books was very good. Clearly he was a man of learning, though his knowledge seems to have been acquired in the Low Countries rather than at Oxford or Cambridge, thus incurring Walpole's disdain.

Sir Richard was said to be a Dissenter, a member of Edmund Calamy's Presbyterian congregation in London. This sits rather oddly with one of the other few known facts about him, for he was a Member of Parliament, first for Grantham, later for Boston. As a Dissenter he should not have been eligible to stand for election. His interest in religious matters is demonstrated by his choice of books. His particular subject was philology, especially the text of the bible: indeed, he published a study of the words and phrases in the New Testament, *Fortuita Sacra*, issued in Rotterdam in 1727. His collection of books includes a Greek lexicon in eleven manuscript volumes compiled by Joannes Caspar Suicerus, and a Latin thesaurus by

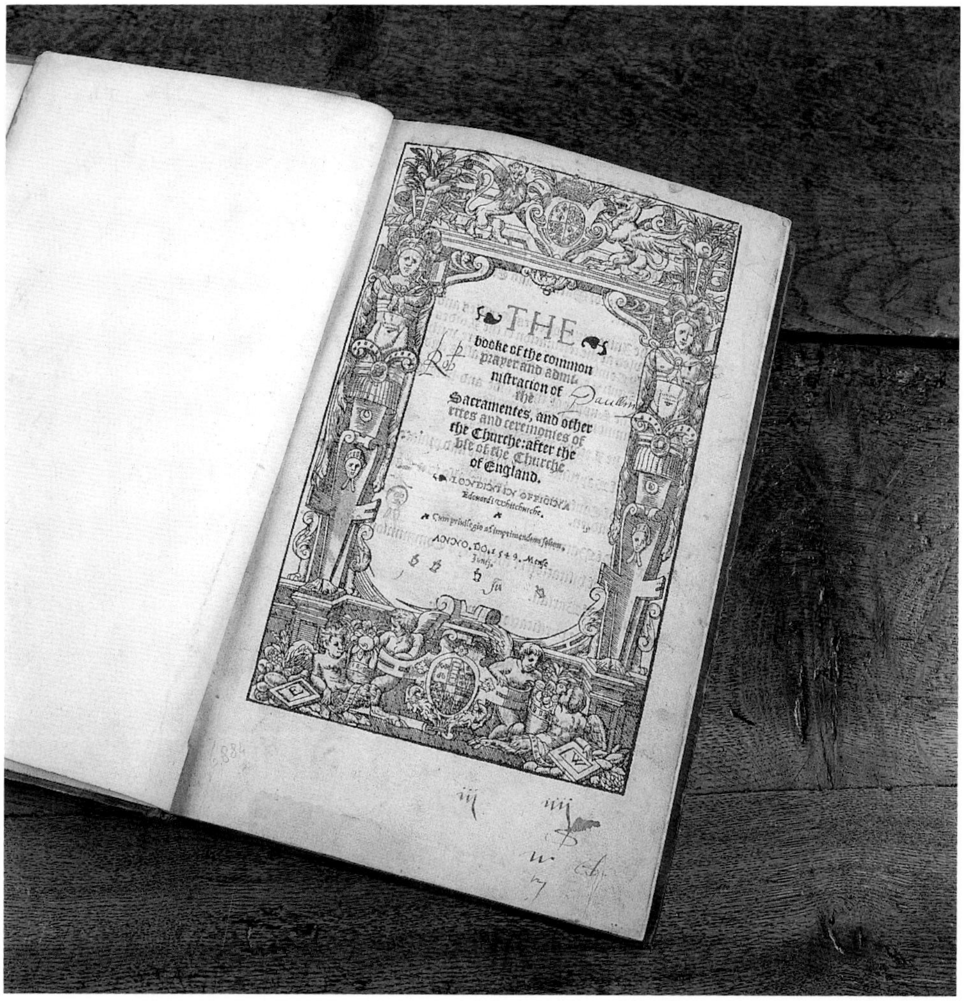

The Book of Common Prayer *printed in English in London in 1549, from Sir Richard Ellys's collection of books at Blickling. (NTPL/Mike Williams)*

Robert Estienne printed on large sheets to allow for revisions. Amongst numerous bibles, are two versions by Miles Coverdale and a 'Red Indian' Bible printed in Cambridge, Massachusetts in 1661–3.

But Sir Richard had interests beyond religion; indeed he had an eye for the antique, the rare and the beautiful. Although two very early English manuscripts – an eighth-century psalter and a tenth-century book of sermons known as the Blickling Homilies – were unfortunately sold in 1932 to pay death duties, the collection still contains over a hundred books printed before 1500, such as work from the Aldine Press in Venice. Products of the early European presses were already rare items in the early eighteenth century, so he was showing discrimination and determination in pursuing them. Fine bindings are superbly represented by seven volumes of *The Digest* printed in Paris in 1527–33, each differently bound by Claude Picques.

Many of the books include fine engravings, such as the 'Cabinet du Roi' which illustrates every aspect of the life of Louis XIV at his palace of Versailles, from the architecture, to the fountains and the tapestries.

Sir Richard employed John Mitchell, who was based in Bolton Street in London, as his librarian and cataloguer. Many of the books at Blickling bear an 'M' on the endpaper, showing that he had examined them. Some have brief bibliographical notes, stating that the plates are all present, or that the binding is imperfect. Mitchell also acted as middleman for the various agents used by Ellys to build up his collection, and they bought on his behalf at the great sales of books in England and on the Continent. One of the most spectacular of these sales was of the library of Edward Harley, Earl of Oxford, at Wimpole Hall in Cambridgeshire. Harley's financial ruin resulted in the sale of first the Wimpole estate in 1739, then of his books and furnishings, a catastrophe that hastened his death in July 1741. Letters written by Ellys at this time show he was preparing to bid, but death overtook him as well.

Eighteenth- and early nineteenth-century guidebooks to Blickling underline the importance of the book collection. Dibdin's *Library Companion* of 1824 describes the various volumes in 'the magnificent old library' and explains how it was run by Rev. Churchill, chaplain to Lady Suffield, Blickling's then owner. In extravagant language Dibdin writes,

> I cannot refrain from indulging in one minute's delightful recollection of the morning, passed within its precincts, when, in company with Atticus, and Marcus, and Petronius, we revelled and rioted midst strange Greek MSS, and quaint printed tomes; a morning followed up by a hospitable carousel at the Tusculum of Mr Churchill. . . .

The Rev. Churchill allowed scholars to browse but resolutely refused to lend, even when a Greek lexicographer claimed he was engaged on a work of national importance.

When Ellys's collection arrived at Blickling, Lord Buckinghamshire had decided to house it in the Long Gallery. He cleared out the full-length portraits lining the walls, replacing them with bookcases. In 1858, when the 8th Lord Lothian inherited the house, he embarked on a programme of redecoration supervised by Benjamin Woodward. Woodward had been working on the interior of the Oxford Union's Debating Hall with William Morris, Edward Burne-Jones, Dante Gabriel Rossetti, Val Prinsep and John Hungerford Pollen. When Lord Lothian asked Woodward to organise the redecoration of the Long Gallery, he incorporated the early eighteenth-century bookcases into new ones with a Gothic profile carved with naturalistic foliage by the O'Shea brothers. Pollen was brought in to paint the frieze above the bookcases. Possibly taking his inspiration from a fifteenth-century edition of Suetonius' *Lives of the Twelve Caesars* from the book collection, he chose as his theme Renaissance white vine coiling round figures of art and literature on a kilim style background.

Despite the loss of the two early English manuscripts, the collection bequeathed to Lord Buckinghamshire is virtually intact, unlike so many country-house libraries which were dispersed or pillaged in the twentieth century. The superb collection of books is still housed in the Jacobean Long Gallery, its plasterwork ceiling appropriately decorated with symbols of the Five Senses and Doctrina, or Learning, from Henry Peacham's book, *Minerva Britanna*, published in 1612. Visitors can admire the bindings of the books in their shelves in the Pre-Raphaelite bookcases, or examine some of the highlights of the library on show in the Document Room at the end of the visitor route. The theme for 1999 is 'Devotion – books of personal religion'.

A Luxurious Academy

George Wyndham, 3rd Earl Egremont, was famous for his hospitality at his country seat, Petworth in Sussex. The painter Thomas Phillips described him as 'my best friend and benefactor, who for forty-one years has never ceased to shew his favour and kindness to me and mine, and whom I and my family have learn't to honour and love as a Father.' Fellow artist Benjamin Robert Haydon was even more rhapsodical, comparing Egremont to the sun: 'The very flies at Petworth seem to know that there is room for their existence, that the windows are theirs.'

Wyndham was only twelve years of age when in 1763 his father suddenly died as a result of over-indulgence, having a particular liking for turtle dinners. The 3rd Earl showed no such frailty, living to the venerable age of eighty-six. His stewardship of Petworth during these long years can be regarded as its golden age. In many ways he was very much the Georgian – a wit, a benevolent landlord, an innovative agriculturalist, friend of leading society figures such as Charles James Fox and Georgiana, Duchess of Devonshire, paying the gambling debts of both. He was also a great gallant, his liaison with Lady Melbourne is said to have produced one Prime Minister, the 2nd Viscount Melbourne, and the wife of another, Lady Palmerston. But he was also fond of a private life; in 1784 he retired to Petworth with his fifteen-year-old mistress, Elizabeth Iliffe, daughter of a Westminster schoolteacher. Calling herself Mrs Wyndham, she bore him seven children. Egremont married Mrs Wyndham in

1801 but this regularisation of the union promptly broke it up, as she could not abide his continuing infidelities.

Lady Spencer maintained,

> [he had] *forty-three* children who all live in the house with him and their respective Mothers; that the latter are usually kept in the background but that when any quarrels arise, which few days pass without, each Mother takes part with her Progeny, bursts into the drawing room, fights with each other, Ld E. and his Children . . . and makes scenes worthy of Billingsgate or a Mad House.

Though a wonderfully exaggerated account, many families did indeed live for extended periods at Petworth. These were the dependants of the artists who enjoyed Egremont's patronage.

Wyndham inherited both a tradition for artistic patronage and a fine art collection. In the seventeenth century, Algernon Percy, 10th Earl of Northumberland, had collected twenty Van Dyck portraits, and through the vicissitudes of the Civil War had acquired Italian masterpieces. Charles Seymour, the Proud Duke of Somerset, had commissioned murals by Laguerre and bought the magnificent Claude, *Landscape with Jacob and Laban*. Wyndham's father, the 2nd Lord Egremont, had acquired Italian and Dutch paintings and a magnificent collection of antique statuary, for which he built the North Gallery at Petworth.

Declaring that he 'looked upon Raphael and Hogarth as the two greatest painters that ever lived' the 3rd Earl at first displayed classic eighteenth-century taste, buying not only works by Hogarth but also Reynolds, and Romney, who was commissioned in 1795 to paint Mrs Wyndham and her children. Elizabeth Wyndham was herself an artist and commissioned two paintings by William Blake, *Satan Calling up his Legions* and *The Last Judgement*.

In 1802 Egremont purchased from the Royal Academy J. M. W. Turner's great painting of ships preparing to drop anchor, known as the *Egremont Seapiece*. The artist was invited to come to treat Petworth as if it were his own home, with a room over the chapel converted into a studio. In return for this generosity, Turner painted landscapes of Petworth, of Cockermouth Castle in Cumbria, home of the medieval Egremonts, of Brighton Chain Pier and the Chichester Canal. He also produced dozens of sketches of the park and of the house interior which provide a wonderfully atmospheric record of early nineteenth-century Petworth.

Turner was now joined in a kind of inner artistic circle at Petworth by William Beechey, Francis Chantrey, Thomas Phillips and C. R. Leslie. From these and other contemporary artists, Egremont liked to commission works of inspiration rather than imitation, telling Leslie 'I wish to keep you employed on such [historical and

The Last Judgement *by William Blake, commissioned by Elizabeth Wyndham. (NTPL/John Hammond)*

literary] subjects instead of portraits'. The North Gallery at Petworth is now filled with pictures reflecting his literary tastes: from Shakespeare, for instance, Henry Fuseli's *Macbeth and the Witches*, James Northcote's *Richard III and the Little Princes*; and from Cervantes' *Don Quixote*, Leslie's representation of *Sancho and the Duchess*.

He also commissioned contemporary sculpture. John Flaxman created the huge piece that still dominates the Square Bay of the North Gallery, *St Michael Overcoming Satan*, inspired by Milton's *Paradise Lost*. This was completed for Egremont in 1826, just as he had finished extending the Gallery to accommodate his commissions as well as the antique statuary he had inherited from his father.

Another sculptor favoured by Egremont was the young Irishman, John Edward Carew, who was regarded by Haydon as 'perhaps the best cutter of marble in England ... but idle in thoughts, preferring the chat of a gossiping Coffee House to the glory of fame'. While he produced the great group *Venus, Vulcan and Cupid*, Carew lived at Petworth and was provided with a studio in Brighton. However, Carew was to bite the hand that fed him, for on Egremont's death in 1837 he sued his executors for £50,000. When he lost the case, he was driven into bankruptcy, fulfilling Egremont's prediction, 'when I'm gone, he'll be a beggar'.

Above a fireplace in the North Gallery hangs Thomas Phillips' portrait, painted two years after Egremont's death for his eldest son, Colonel George Wyndham. It shows Egremont seated in the Gallery with various works of art from his collection in the background, including Turner's *Egremont Seapiece*, Leslie's *Sancho and the Duchess*, Flaxman's *St Michael*, and, to one side, perhaps to reflect his ingratitude, Carew's *Venus, Vulcan and Cupid*. But this is not just a record of a great collector, it is also a tribute to a kind and generous man described by the diarist Creevey as 'an extraordinary person, perhaps as any in England, certainly the most so of his caste or order'.

Mrs Ronnie Greville with His Highness, the Maharajah of Mysore, photographed in the Rose Garden at Polesden Lacey in 1938. (NT/Rupert Truman)

Red Carpets, Fine Collections

There was nothing half-hearted about Mrs Ronnie Greville, society hostess and chatelaine of Polesden Lacey in Surrey. While her friends praised her generosity and hospitality, her enemies voiced their dislike in no uncertain terms. Cecil Beaton described her as 'a galumphing, greedy, snobbish old toad who watered her chops at the sight of royalty and the Prince of Wales' set and did nothing for anybody except the rich.' She in her turn could give as good as she got. Her dismissal of fellow soci-

ety lioness Emerald Cunard combined her sharp tongue with that very love of royalty: 'You mustn't think that I dislike little Lady Cunard. I'm always telling Queen Mary that she isn't half as bad as she is painted.'

Mrs Greville's life was one long act of defiance. She was the illegitimate daughter and only child of the brewer William McEwan and a woman variously described as his housekeeper, cook and wife of his day porter. Father and daughter were very close, so the chief figure in her upbringing was a self-made, plain-speaking millionaire: Maggie took her lead from him.

In 1891 she married the Hon. Ronald Greville. Her declaration that she would rather be a beeress than a peeress does not entirely ring true, as she became an avid collector of titled friends. But Greville, described by his wife's god-daughter as a charming and unambitious man, was a close friend of the Prince of Wales who became Edward VII, so he was admirably placed to introduce his wife to the highest echelons of society. With a London house in fashionable Mayfair, and a delightful country villa, a gift from her father, at Polesden Lacey, she embarked upon her career as a society hostess.

Ronnie Greville died in 1908, Edward VII in 1910, but Maggie, now launched firmly in society, was able to sail serenely on. Her hospitality was famous – excellent food and fine wines in superb surroundings. The visitors' and parties books at Polesden Lacey recall those she entertained, including many of the crowned heads of Europe and beyond. The Queen of Spain, the King and Queen of Italy, King Fuad of Egypt and the British royal family all make their appearance, and in 1923 Mrs Greville lent Polesden Lacey to the Duke and Duchess of York, the future George VI and Queen Elizabeth, for their honeymoon. One of her most arresting remarks was, 'One uses up *so* many red carpets in a season!'.

But stormier waters came with the 1930s. Passionately anti-Bolshevik, Maggie Greville, like Lady Astor at Cliveden, entertained high-ranking Nazis including the German Ambassador, Ribbentrop. Harold Nicolson expressed his concern: 'The harm which these silly, selfish hostesses do is really immense. They convey to foreign envoys the impression that policy is decided in their own drawing rooms.' The outbreak of war in 1939 therefore came as a tremendous blow to Mrs Greville. Taking to her wheelchair, she moved into the Dorchester Hotel. Here on 30 April 1942 the diarist and supreme snob, 'Chips' Channon, attended her last great lunch party, recording that 'the old lady received me, covered with jewels, sitting in her bathchair'. He then went on to list the guests: the Earl and Countess Mountbatten, Prince Philip of Greece (now the Duke of Edinburgh), the Duke and Duchess of Kent, the Duchess of Buccleuch, and the Duke of Alba.

This was Maggie Greville's swansong. Four months later she was dead, leaving her jewels to Queen Elizabeth, bequests to Princess Margaret, the Queen of Spain, and various animal charities. Polesden Lacey, her London house and her collections were given to the National Trust. Over the years, she had built up fine collections of porcelain, pictures, furniture and silver to provide the magnificent backdrop for her life as a society hostess. The decor at her house in London adopted the late eighteenth-century style of Louis XVI, while at Polesden Lacey she pursued a more eclectic approach, such as the Jacobean Picture Corridor, where she probably arranged her early Italian, French and Dutch pictures with her sixteenth-century French furniture and her exquisite collection of Italian Renaissance maiolica – tin-glazed earthenware.

The name maiolica is derived from the Italian for Majorca, and applied originally to Islamic pottery imported via the island. By the sixteenth century it was being made in Italy itself, particularly in the area around the Duchy of Urbino. Early pieces, made at Deruta, are patterned in the strong blues, yellows and oranges that are the hallmark of maiolica. Later, in the 1520s and 1530s, the work of mural and easel painters influenced the potters, producing *istoriato* or narrative scenes. A plate at Polesden Lacey shows a scene based on Raphael's depiction of *The Judgement of Paris*.

Mrs Greville's maiolica collection is small, just 34 pieces, but they are all of high quality. She received expert advice from Henry 'Bogey' Harris, a frequent visitor to both the Charles Street London house and Polesden from 1908 onwards. Harris, a member of the Marlborough House Set, had lost much of his fortune playing baccarat with the Prince of Wales, and retired to Italy where he built up a fine art collection. Although not himself a great snob, he became a fervent supporter of Mrs Greville, declaring, 'One can live without everyone really; everyone but Maggie; she's like dram drinking.'

Five *istoriato* plates from Harris's maiolica collection are now at Polesden Lacey. He also introduced the art historian, Professor Tancred Borenius, who features in the Polesden Lacey visitors' books from 1919. Kenneth Clark, later Lord Clark (of 'Civilisation'), recalled Borenius as 'a good scholar, a pleasant companion, and a passionate upholder of the concept of monarchy', which must have endeared him to Maggie Greville. He certainly advised her on purchases of maiolica and may have bought for her, as eight pieces now at Polesden were acquired by him, including the *Judgement of Paris* plate, in a great sale in 1925.

Mrs Greville's maiolica collection is not representative of the genre, but was gathered to provide a decorative ensemble in a cabinet. This now stands at the top of the stairs in the entrance hall at Polesden Lacey. The red carpets are still there too, now trodden by visitors as they admire her fine collections.

DECEMBER – JANUARY

28 MONDAY

29 TUESDAY

30 WEDNESDAY

31 THURSDAY

NEW YEAR'S EVE

1 FRIDAY

NEW YEAR'S DAY
BANK HOLIDAY (UK & EIRE)

2 SATURDAY

3 SUNDAY

JANUARY

4 MONDAY BANK HOLIDAY (SCOTLAND)

5 TUESDAY

6 WEDNESDAY EPIPHANY

7 THURSDAY

8 FRIDAY

9 SATURDAY

10 SUNDAY

Cumbrian farmhouse under snow at Loughrigg Tarn, Great Langdale. (NTPL/John Kay)

JANUARY

11 MONDAY

12 TUESDAY

13 WEDNESDAY

14 THURSDAY

15 FRIDAY

16 SATURDAY

17 SUNDAY

Hill Top, the farmhouse at Near Sawrey purchased by Beatrix Potter in 1905. (NTPL/Stephen Robson)

JANUARY

18 MONDAY MARTIN LUTHER KING'S BIRTHDAY OBSERVED (US)

19 TUESDAY

20 WEDNESDAY

21 THURSDAY

22 FRIDAY

23 SATURDAY

24 SUNDAY

Wall End Farm with Great Langdale behind. (NTPL/Robert Thrift)

JANUARY

25 MONDAY

26 TUESDAY

27 WEDNESDAY

28 THURSDAY

29 FRIDAY

30 SATURDAY

31 SUNDAY

Mr D. Birkett with Herdwicks at Yew Tree Farm, part of the Monk Coniston estate. (NTPL)

FEBRUARY

1 MONDAY

2 TUESDAY

3 WEDNESDAY

4 THURSDAY

5 FRIDAY

6 SATURDAY

7 SUNDAY

A seventeenth-century chair of estate and footstool in the Leicester Gallery at Knole. James I, seated in just such a chair, looks down upon the furniture – an appropriate gesture, for he and his successors were the sources of the magnificent collection that is now one of the glories of the house. (NTPL/ Andreas von Einsiedel)

FEBRUARY

8 MONDAY

9 TUESDAY

10 WEDNESDAY

11 THURSDAY

12 FRIDAY

13 SATURDAY

14 SUNDAY ST VALENTINE'S DAY

The state bed in the King's Bedroom at Knole. This bed, and its accompanying chairs and stools, was probably made by the French upholsterer, Jean Peyrard, for the wedding of James, Duke of York, and Mary of Modena in 1673. (NTPL/Andreas von Einsiedel)

FEBRUARY

15 MONDAY PRESIDENT'S DAY (US)

16 TUESDAY SHROVE TUESDAY

17 WEDNESDAY ASH WEDNESDAY (LENT BEGINS)

18 THURSDAY

19 FRIDAY

20 SATURDAY

21 SUNDAY FIRST SUNDAY OF LENT

A detail from the tester of the state bed in the Venetian Ambassador's Room at Knole. Putti support the monogram of James II, showing that this bed was made for the King in 1688, shortly before his flight from England. (NTPL/Andreas von Einsiedel)

FEBRUARY

22 MONDAY

23 TUESDAY

24 WEDNESDAY

25 THURSDAY

26 FRIDAY

27 SATURDAY

28 SUNDAY

The King's Closet at Knole. In the right-hand foreground is a close stool encased in red velvet – one of the more curious perks acquired by Charles Sackville from the Stuart kings. (NTPL/Andreas von Einsiedel)

MARCH

1 MONDAY ST DAVID'S DAY

2 TUESDAY

3 WEDNESDAY

4 THURSDAY

5 FRIDAY

6 SATURDAY

7 SUNDAY

A detail from one of the gentleman's court coats collected by Charles Paget Wade. This example, dating from the 1770s, is made of striped velvet covered in lavish embroidery. (NTPL/Andreas von Einsiedel)

MARCH

8 MONDAY

9 TUESDAY

10 WEDNESDAY

11 THURSDAY

12 FRIDAY

13 SATURDAY

14 SUNDAY

FOURTH SUNDAY OF LENT
MOTHER'S DAY (UK)

A late eighteenth-century cotton dress from the Snowshill Collection. Technological developments had made possible the printing of patterns on a washable fabric, marking a true revolution in the history of dress. (NTPL/Andreas von Einsiedel)

MARCH

15 MONDAY

16 TUESDAY

17 WEDNESDAY

ST PATRICK'S DAY
BANK HOLIDAY (NORTHERN IRELAND & EIRE)

18 THURSDAY

19 FRIDAY

20 SATURDAY

21 SUNDAY

FIFTH SUNDAY OF LENT (PASSION SUNDAY)

Some of the early eighteenth-century accessories in the Killerton Collection: a quilted pink satin petticoat; shoes in brocade with their matching protective overshoes; and an Italian fan. (NTPL/Andreas von Einsiedel)

MARCH

22 MONDAY

23 TUESDAY

24 WEDNESDAY

25 THURSDAY
ANNUNCIATION (LADY DAY)

26 FRIDAY

27 SATURDAY

28 SUNDAY
PALM SUNDAY
BRITISH SUMMER TIME BEGINS

A corset from a late nineteenth-century shop display. The flags of the United Kingdom and France are shown together – the Gallic connection would have reassured customers that the finest French fabrics were used to make corsets as 'easy fitting as a perfectly cut kid glove'. (NTPL/Andreas von Einsiedel)

THE
Celebrated CB Corsets
CORSETS DE PREMIÈRE QUALITÉ
SOIGNÉS À LA DERNIÈRE MODE

MARCH – APRIL

29 MONDAY

30 TUESDAY

31 WEDNESDAY

1 THURSDAY

MAUNDY THURSDAY
FIRST DAY OF PASSOVER

2 FRIDAY

GOOD FRIDAY
BANK HOLIDAY (UK & EIRE)

3 SATURDAY

4 SUNDAY

EASTER SUNDAY

Oncidium lanceanum, *an illustration from* Transactions of the Horticultural Society. *Specimens of this orchid were brought back from British Guiana by Thomas Colley in 1834, and presented to James Bateman, then an undergraduate at Oxford. (The Lindley Library)*

Drake, del.

Oncidium Lanceanum.

APRIL

5 MONDAY EASTER MONDAY
BANK HOLIDAY (UK & EIRE)

6 TUESDAY

7 WEDNESDAY

8 THURSDAY

9 FRIDAY

10 SATURDAY

11 SUNDAY

The Chinese Garden at Biddulph Grange. In the centre of the picture is a Japanese maple, Acer japonicum rubeum, *and on the left the venerable golden larch,* Pseudolarix amabilis, *sent from China to England in a Wardian case by Robert Fortune in 1852. (NTPL/Ian Shaw)*

APRIL

12 MONDAY

13 TUESDAY

14 WEDNESDAY

15 THURSDAY

16 FRIDAY

17 SATURDAY

18 SUNDAY

Rhododendron batemani, *named in honour of James Bateman by Dr Joseph Hooker. It flowered at Biddulph Grange in 1863 and was then presented to the Royal Botanic Gardens at Kew. This illustration is from* Curtis's Botanical Magazine. *(The Lindley Library)*

tch, del. et lith.

Vincent Brooks, Imp.

APRIL

19 MONDAY

20 TUESDAY

21 WEDNESDAY

22 THURSDAY

23 FRIDAY ST GEORGE'S DAY

24 SATURDAY

25 SUNDAY

A hardy hybrid rhododendron flourishing in the microclimate of the Glen at Biddulph Grange. (NTPL/Ian Shaw)

APRIL – MAY

26 MONDAY

27 TUESDAY

28 WEDNESDAY

29 THURSDAY

30 FRIDAY

1 SATURDAY

2 SUNDAY

A wildfowling scene from a Theban tomb, one of the copies commissioned by William Bankes from various artists during his expeditions to Egypt. (NTPL/Derrick E. Witty)

MAY

3 MONDAY BANK HOLIDAY (UK & EIRE)

4 TUESDAY

5 WEDNESDAY

6 THURSDAY

7 FRIDAY

8 SATURDAY

9 SUNDAY MOTHER'S DAY (US)

A plate from La Description l'Egypte 1809–28, *showing the west temple at Thebes. The book is now in the Egyptian collection at Kingston Lacy. (NTPL/ Derrick E. Witty)*

MAY

10 MONDAY

11 TUESDAY

12 WEDNESDAY

13 THURSDAY ASCENSION DAY

14 FRIDAY

15 SATURDAY

16 SUNDAY SUNDAY AFTER ASCENSION

The Spanish Room at Kingston Lacy, vicariously created by William John Bankes during his exile in Italy to exhibit his collection of Spanish paintings. The lavishly gilt and coffered ceiling and the tooled and leather hangings on the walls were bought from Venetian palaces. (NTPL/James Mortimer)

MAY

17 MONDAY

18 TUESDAY

19 WEDNESDAY

28 THURSDAY

21 FRIDAY

22 SATURDAY

23 SUNDAY WHIT SUNDAY (PENTECOST)

Portrait of Don Francisco Vives de Cañamas, Conde de Faura, painted by the seventeenth-century artist, Jerónimo Jacinto de Espinosa. William John Bankes bought the painting in 1814 during his visit to Spain. (NTPL/Christopher Hurst)

MAY

24 MONDAY

25 TUESDAY

26 WEDNESDAY

27 THURSDAY

28 FRIDAY

29 SATURDAY

30 SUNDAY TRINITY SUNDAY

Detail of Winter, one of the pietra dura *panels of the seasons decorating a cabinet in the Spanish Room. These were commissioned by Bankes from the Buoninsegni brothers in Florence in 1850. (NTPL/Richard Pink)*

MAY – JUNE

31 MONDAY BANK HOLIDAY (UK)
MEMORIAL DAY (US)

1 TUESDAY

2 WEDNESDAY

3 THURSDAY

4 FRIDAY

5 SATURDAY

6 SUNDAY

One of the embroidered wall hangings made in applied work for Bess of Hardwick, c.1573. This detail shows Penelope, the faithful wife of Ulysses, with whom Bess identified herself. (NTPL/John Hammond)

PENELOPE

JUNE

7 MONDAY BANK HOLIDAY (EIRE)

8 TUESDAY

9 WEDNESDAY

10 THURSDAY

11 FRIDAY

12 SATURDAY

13 SUNDAY

One of a series of late sixteenth-century Brussels tapestries of gods and planets in the Blue Room at Hardwick. This panel shows Cybele in her chariot being pulled by two lions. (NTPL/John Hammond)

JUNE

14 MONDAY

15 TUESDAY

16 WEDNESDAY

17 THURSDAY

18 FRIDAY

19 SATURDAY

20 SUNDAY FATHER'S DAY (UK & US)

A detail of Pan playing the bagpipes from the corner of one of the gods and planets tapestries in the Blue Room at Hardwick. (NTPL/John Hammond)

JUNE

21 MONDAY MIDSUMMER'S DAY – THE LONGEST DAY

22 TUESDAY

23 WEDNESDAY

24 THURSDAY

25 FRIDAY

26 SATURDAY

27 SUNDAY

An embroidery panel in red velvet decorated with silver strapwork, with the initials ES for Elizabeth, Countess of Shrewsbury. (NTPL/John Hammond)

ES

JUNE – JULY

28 MONDAY

29 TUESDAY

30 WEDNESDAY

1 THURSDAY

2 FRIDAY

3 SATURDAY

4 SUNDAY

Central detail of a table carpet of English Turkey work in the Paved Room. The Judgement of Paris *is framed by the Hardwick stags, Bess's arms and dated 1574. (NTPL/John Bethell)*

1574
S

JULY

5 MONDAY INDEPENDENCE DAY OBSERVED (US)

6 TUESDAY

7 WEDNESDAY

8 THURSDAY

9 FRIDAY

10 SATURDAY

11 SUNDAY

The Clive Museum at Powis, housed in the ballroom range. (NTPL/Tim Beddow)

JULY

12 MONDAY BANK HOLIDAY (NORTHERN IRELAND)

13 TUESDAY

14 WEDNESDAY

15 THURSDAY

16 FRIDAY

17 SATURDAY

18 SUNDAY

A detail from Tipu's chintz tent, made in the later Mughal period, c.1725–50. When the tent was brought back to Powis by the 2nd Lord Clive, it was used for many years as a marquee for garden parties. (Courtesy of the Earl of Powis and the Powis Estate Trustees)

JULY

19 MONDAY

20 TUESDAY

21 WEDNESDAY

22 THURSDAY

23 FRIDAY

24 SATURDAY

25 SUNDAY

Tiger-head finial in gold, set with rubies, diamonds and emeralds, from the golden throne of Tipu Sultan. The throne was broken up after the fall of Tipu in May 1799, and the finial, one of only two to survive, was presented to Edward, 2nd Lord Clive. (NTPL/Erik Pelham)

JULY – AUGUST

26 MONDAY

27 TUESDAY

28 WEDNESDAY

29 THURSDAY

30 FRIDAY

31 SATURDAY

1 SUNDAY

The Saloon at Calke Abbey, filled with glazed cases containing various pieces from the family's natural history collections, including stuffed animals and birds, shells, fossils and, in the foreground, the skull of an alligator. (NTPL/Michael Freeman)

AUGUST

2 MONDAY BANK HOLIDAY (SCOTLAND & EIRE)

3 TUESDAY

4 WEDNESDAY

5 THURSDAY

6 FRIDAY

7 SATURDAY

8 SUNDAY

The Bird Lobby, with some of the stuffed bird collection built up by Sir John Harpur Crewe and his son, Vauncey. (NTPL/Michael Freeman)

AUGUST

9 MONDAY

10 TUESDAY

11 WEDNESDAY

12 THURSDAY

13 FRIDAY

14 SATURDAY

15 SUNDAY

Sir Vauncey Harpur Crewe's collection of bird's eggs. (NTPL/Michael Freeman)

THE FAMILY B
CONTAINING ONE DOZEN LARGE TA
YARDLEY & CO'S
IMPERIAL WINDSOR SOA
PRICE FIVE SHILLINGS AND SIXPENCE.
Manufactory—Ridgemount Street, Store Street, TOTTENHAM COURT ROAD LONDON W.C.
Glossy Ibis
HABANA
TABACOS PUROS
DE LA VUELTA ABAJO

AUGUST

16 MONDAY

17 TUESDAY

18 WEDNESDAY

19 THURSDAY

20 FRIDAY

21 SATURDAY

22 SUNDAY

Sir Vauncey Harpur Crewe's bedroom at Calke Abbey, with some of his natural history collections amid the chaos. (NTPL/Christopher Dalton)

AUGUST

23 MONDAY

24 TUESDAY

25 WEDNESDAY

26 THURSDAY

27 FRIDAY

28 SATURDAY

29 SUNDAY

Detail of the auricula theatre installed in the Flower Garden at Calke in the early nineteenth century by Georgina, Lady Crewe. (NTPL/Stephen Robson)

AUGUST – SEPTEMBER

30 MONDAY BANK HOLIDAY (UK, EXCEPT SCOTLAND)

31 TUESDAY

1 WEDNESDAY

2 THURSDAY

3 FRIDAY

4 SATURDAY

5 SUNDAY

The Staircase Hall at Arlington Court, a watercolour painted c.1914 by Chrissie Peters, companion to Rosalie Chichester. Some of Miss Chichester's collection of stuffed animals can be seen in the hall, and items from her pewter collection on the landing bookcases. (NTPL/John Hammond)

SEPTEMBER

6 MONDAY LABOR DAY (US)

7 TUESDAY

8 WEDNESDAY

9 THURSDAY

10 FRIDAY

11 SATURDAY ROSH HASHANAH

12 SUNDAY

Model ships from the Arlington collection; many of the early nineteenth-century examples were made by French prisoners of war. (NTPL/Nadia MacKenzie)

SEPTEMBER

13 MONDAY

14 TUESDAY

15 WEDNESDAY

16 THURSDAY

17 FRIDAY

18 SATURDAY

19 SUNDAY

Detail from an early nineteenth-century scrap screen in the Staircase Hall at Arlington. Young ladies would collect prints and engravings and pass wet afternoons cutting them out and sticking them on screens, which could then be used to keep draughts at bay. (NTPL/John Hammond)

Drawn by M.E.
HOW AR' YE OFF FOR FISH
Cruikshank fec.t
The Cholic
Pub.d Feb.y 12 1819 by G Humphrey. 27 S.t James's S.t
FISHERMAN,

SEPTEMBER

20 MONDAY DAY OF ATONEMENT (YOM KIPPUR)

21 TUESDAY

22 WEDNESDAY

23 THURSDAY

24 FRIDAY

25 SATURDAY

26 SUNDAY

Fans, parasols, jewellery, trinkets and souvenirs of the Chichester family, mounted by Jan Newman in one of the cabinets in the Lobby at Arlington. (NTPL/Nadia MacKenzie)

SEPTEMBER – OCTOBER

27 MONDAY

28 TUESDAY

29 WEDNESDAY MICHAELMAS DAY

30 THURSDAY

1 FRIDAY

2 SATURDAY

3 SUNDAY

The Long Gallery at Blickling, with Sir Richard Ellys's collection of books displayed in cases along the walls. Above the bookcases is the coiling vine frieze painted by John Hungerford Pollen. (NTPL/Nadia MacKenzie)

OCTOBER

4 MONDAY

5 TUESDAY

6 WEDNESDAY

7 THURSDAY

8 FRIDAY

9 SATURDAY

10 SUNDAY

Pages from a fifteenth-century edition of Suetonius' Lives of the Twelve Caesars, *showing the design that probably inspired Pollen's decoration for the frieze in the Long Gallery at Blickling. (NTPL/Horst Kolo)*

GAII SVETONII TRANQVILLI DE VITA CAESARVM
LIBER PRIMVS EXPLICIT.
INCIPIT. DIVVS AVGVSTVS LIBER SECVNDVS FAELICI

GENTEM. OCTAVIAM VE
litris precipuam olim fuisse
multa declarant. Nam et
vicus celeberrima parte op
pidi iam pridem octavius
vocabatur. et ostendebatur
ara octavio consecrata. qui bel
lo dux finitimo cum forte
marti rem divinam faceret. nuntiata repente hostis
incursione semicruda exta rapta foco prosecutus. atque
ita prelium ingressus victor redit. decretum etiam publicum
extabat quo cavetur ut in posterum quoque simili modo exta
marti redderentur. reliquie ad octavios referrentur. Ea
gens a tarquinio prisco rege inter minores gentes adlec

Romanas

OCTOBER

11 MONDAY COLUMBUS DAY (US)

12 TUESDAY

13 WEDNESDAY

14 THURSDAY

15 FRIDAY

16 SATURDAY

17 SUNDAY

Poppies from an early seventeenth-century florilegium, Columna's Icones*: the impression of the leaves is produced by pressing inked specimens. (NTPL/Mike Williams)*

[Pa]pauer Rhoeas sylvestre agrorum.

OCTOBER

18 MONDAY

19 TUESDAY

20 WEDNESDAY

21 THURSDAY

22 FRIDAY

23 SATURDAY

24 SUNDAY

The seven volumes of The Digest *printed in Paris between 1527 and 1533, each superbly bound with individual designs by Claude Picques. (NTPL/Mike Williams)*

OCTOBER

25 MONDAY BANK HOLIDAY (EIRE)

26 TUESDAY

27 WEDNESDAY

28 THURSDAY

29 FRIDAY

30 SATURDAY

31 SUNDAY BRITISH SUMMER TIME ENDS
HALLOWE'EN

Detail from the plaster ceiling of the Long Gallery at Blickling, showing Pulchritudo Fominea from Henry Peacham's Minerva Britanna, *published in 1612. (NTPL/Nadia MacKenzie)*

PVLCHRITVDO FOEMINEA

NOVEMBER

1 MONDAY ALL SAINTS' DAY

2 TUESDAY

3 WEDNESDAY

4 THURSDAY

5 FRIDAY GUY FAWKES' NIGHT

6 SATURDAY

7 SUNDAY

George Wyndham, 3rd Earl of Egremont, in a posthumous portrait by Thomas Phillips, one of a number of artists who enjoyed the Earl's hospitality and patronage. He has depicted his benefactor in the North Gallery with various works of art from his collection in the background. (NTPL/John Hammond)

NOVEMBER

8 MONDAY

9 TUESDAY

10 WEDNESDAY

11 THURSDAY VETERANS' DAY (US)

12 FRIDAY

13 SATURDAY

14 SUNDAY REMEMBRANCE SUNDAY

Princess Bridget Plantagenet dedicated to the Nunnery at Dartford, *by James Northcote, one of a series of paintings with historic themes commissioned by Lord Egremont. (NTPL/Derrick E. Witty)*

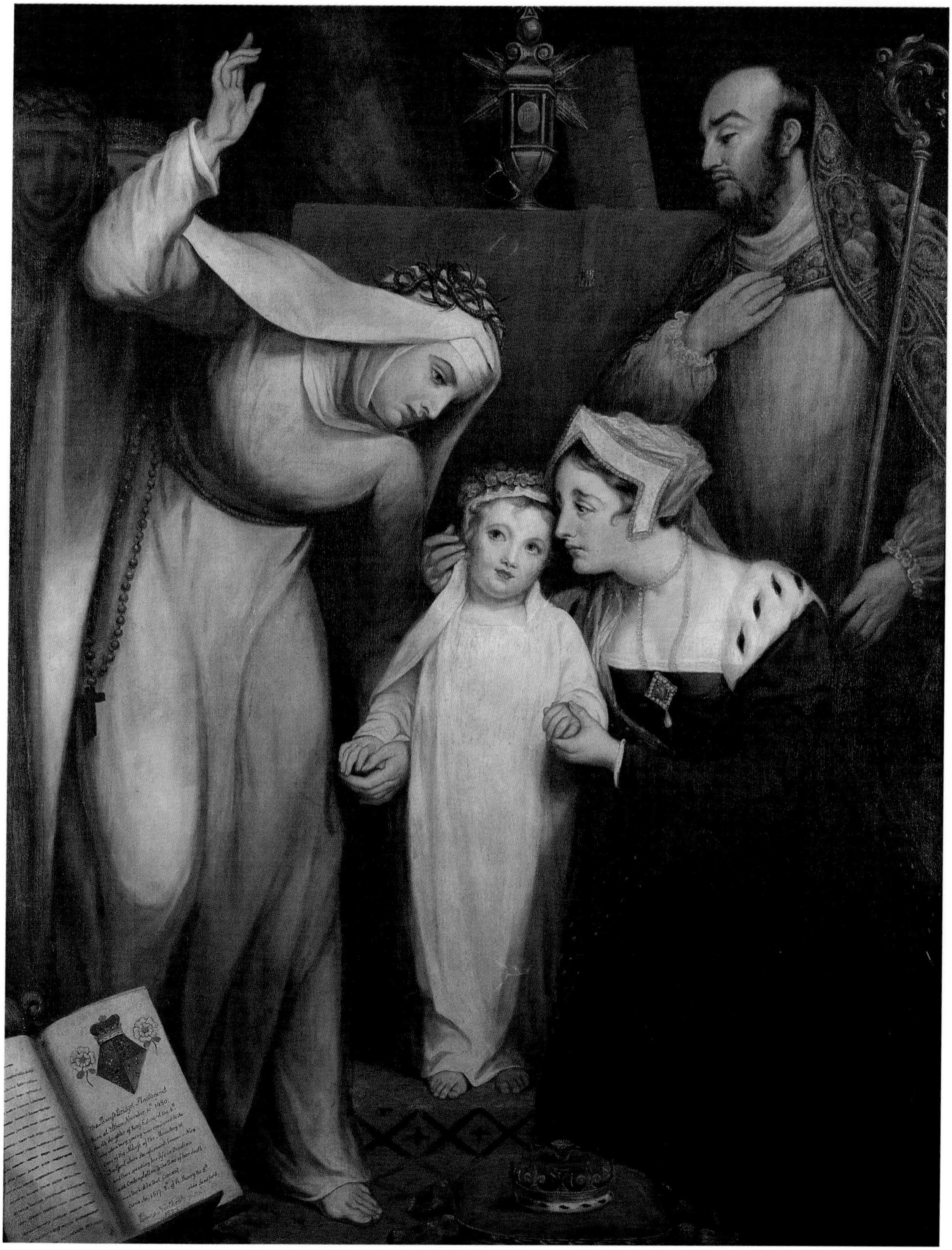
The Princess Bridget Plantagenet
Born at Eltham November 10th 1480,
daughter of King Edward the 4th
Abbess of the Monastery at
Dartford where she afterwards became a Nun
and there spending her life in Devotion
and Contemplation to the time of her death
was buried in that Convent.
Circa An. 1517. 8th of K. Henry the 8th
vide Sandford.

NOVEMBER

15 MONDAY

16 TUESDAY

17 WEDNESDAY

18 THURSDAY

19 FRIDAY

20 SATURDAY

21 SUNDAY

Macbeth and the Witches, *a Shakespearean theme as interpreted by Henry Fuseli for Lord Egremont. (NTPL/Derrick E. Witty)*

NOVEMBER

22 MONDAY

23 TUESDAY

24 WEDNESDAY

25 THURSDAY THANKSGIVING DAY (US)

26 FRIDAY

27 SATURDAY

28 SUNDAY FIRST SUNDAY IN ADVENT

The Square Bay of the North Gallery at Petworth, with John Flaxman's dramatic sculpture of St Michael Overcoming Satan, *surrounded by statues worked for Lord Egremont by the Irish sculptor, John Edward Carew. (NTPL/Andreas von Einsiedel)*

NOVEMBER – DECEMBER

29 MONDAY

30 TUESDAY ST ANDREW'S DAY

1 WEDNESDAY

2 THURSDAY

3 FRIDAY

4 SATURDAY HANUKKAH

5 SUNDAY

Busts and a statue from the collection of antique sculpture gathered by Charles Wyndham, 2nd Earl of Egremont, now in the South Corridor of the North Gallery at Petworth. (NTPL/Andreas von Einsiedel)

DECEMBER

6 MONDAY

7 TUESDAY

8 WEDNESDAY

9 THURSDAY

10 FRIDAY

11 SATURDAY

12 SUNDAY

The Jacobean Corridor at Polesden Lacey, with Carolus-Duran's portrait of Mrs Ronnie Greville, painted in 1891. (NTPL/Andreas von Einsiedel)

DECEMBER

13 MONDAY

14 TUESDAY

15 WEDNESDAY

16 THURSDAY

17 FRIDAY

18 SATURDAY

19 SUNDAY

An istoriato *maiolica plate, dating from the 1520s or '30s showing* The Judgement of Paris *after a drawing by Raphael. (NTPL/Andreas von Einsiedel)*

DECEMBER

20 MONDAY

21 TUESDAY

22 WEDNESDAY THE SHORTEST DAY

23 THURSDAY

24 FRIDAY CHRISTMAS EVE

25 SATURDAY CHRISTMAS DAY

26 SUNDAY BOXING DAY

A Deruta plate from Mrs Greville's maiolica collection, showing the profile of a man surrounded by running hounds. (NTPL/Andreas von Einsiedel)

DECEMBER – JANUARY

27 MONDAY BANK HOLIDAY (UK & EIRE)

28 TUESDAY BANK HOLIDAY (UK & EIRE)

29 WEDNESDAY

30 THURSDAY

31 FRIDAY NEW YEAR'S EVE

1 SATURDAY NEW YEAR'S DAY

2 SUNDAY

Maiolica birds, a hawk and a parrot, made in Urbino, c.1570. (NTPL/Andreas von Einsiedel)

1998

	JANUARY	FEBRUARY	MARCH	APRIL	MAY	JUNE
Monday	5 12 19 26	2 9 16 23	2 9 16 23 30	6 13 20 27	4 11 18 25	1 8 15 22 29
Tuesday	6 13 20 27	3 10 17 24	3 10 17 24 31	7 14 21 28	5 12 19 26	2 9 16 23 30
Wednesday	7 14 21 28	4 11 18 25	4 11 18 25	1 8 15 22 29	6 13 20 27	3 10 17 24
Thursday	1 8 15 22 29	5 12 19 26	5 12 19 26	2 9 16 23 30	7 14 21 28	4 11 18 25
Friday	2 9 16 23 30	6 13 20 27	6 13 20 27	3 10 17 24	1 8 15 22 29	5 12 19 26
Saturday	3 10 17 24 31	7 14 21 28	7 14 21 28	4 11 18 25	2 9 16 23 30	6 13 20 27
Sunday	4 11 18 25	1 8 15 22	1 8 15 22 29	5 12 19 26	3 10 17 24 31	7 14 21 28

	JULY	AUGUST	SEPTEMBER	OCTOBER	NOVEMBER	DECEMBER
Monday	6 13 20 27	3 10 17 24 31	7 14 21 28	5 12 19 26	2 9 16 23 30	7 14 21 28
Tuesday	7 14 21 28	4 11 18 25	1 8 15 22 29	6 13 20 27	3 10 17 24	1 8 15 22 29
Wednesday	1 8 15 22 29	5 12 19 26	2 9 16 23 30	7 14 21 28	4 11 18 25	2 9 16 23 30
Thursday	2 9 16 23 30	6 13 20 27	3 10 17 24	1 8 15 22 29	5 12 19 26	3 10 17 24 31
Friday	3 10 17 24 31	7 14 21 28	4 11 18 25	2 9 16 23 30	6 13 20 27	4 11 18 25
Saturday	4 11 18 25	1 8 15 22 29	5 12 19 26	3 10 17 24 31	7 14 21 28	5 12 19 26
Sunday	5 12 19 26	2 9 16 23 30	6 13 20 27	4 11 18 25	1 8 15 22 29	6 13 20 27

1999

	JANUARY	FEBRUARY	MARCH	APRIL	MAY	JUNE
Monday	4 11 18 25	1 8 15 22	1 8 15 22 29	5 12 19 26	3 10 17 24 31	7 14 21 28
Tuesday	5 12 19 26	2 9 16 23	2 9 16 23 30	6 13 20 27	4 11 18 25	1 8 15 22 29
Wednesday	6 13 20 27	3 10 17 24	3 10 17 24 31	7 14 21 28	5 12 19 26	2 9 16 23 30
Thursday	7 14 21 28	4 11 18 25	4 11 18 25	1 8 15 22 29	6 13 20 27	3 10 17 24
Friday	1 8 15 22 29	5 12 19 26	5 12 19 26	2 9 16 23 30	7 14 21 28	4 11 18 25
Saturday	2 9 16 23 30	6 13 20 27	6 13 20 27	3 10 17 24	1 8 15 22 29	5 12 19 26
Sunday	3 10 17 24 31	7 14 21 28	7 14 21 28	4 11 18 25	2 9 16 23 30	6 13 20 27

	JULY	AUGUST	SEPTEMBER	OCTOBER	NOVEMBER	DECEMBER
Monday	5 12 19 26	2 9 16 23 30	6 13 20 27	4 11 18 25	1 8 15 22 29	6 13 20 27
Tuesday	6 13 20 27	3 10 17 24 31	7 14 21 28	5 12 19 26	2 9 16 23 30	7 14 21 28
Wednesday	7 14 21 28	4 11 18 25	1 8 15 22 29	6 13 20 27	3 10 17 24	1 8 15 22 29
Thursday	1 8 15 22 29	5 12 19 26	2 9 16 23 30	7 14 21 28	4 11 18 25	2 9 16 23 30
Friday	2 9 16 23 30	6 13 20 27	3 10 17 24	1 8 15 22 29	5 12 19 26	3 10 17 24 31
Saturday	3 10 17 24 31	7 14 21 28	4 11 18 25	2 9 16 23 30	6 13 20 27	4 11 18 25
Sunday	4 11 18 25	1 8 15 22 29	5 12 19 26	3 10 17 24 31	7 14 21 28	5 12 19 26

2000

	JANUARY	FEBRUARY	MARCH	APRIL	MAY	JUNE
Monday	3 10 17 24 31	7 14 21 28	6 13 20 27	3 10 17 24	1 8 15 22 29	5 12 19 26
Tuesday	4 11 18 25	1 8 15 22 29	7 14 21 28	4 11 18 25	2 9 16 23 30	6 13 20 27
Wednesday	5 12 19 26	2 9 16 23	1 8 15 22 29	5 12 19 26	3 10 17 24 31	7 14 21 28
Thursday	6 13 20 27	3 10 17 24	2 9 16 23 30	6 13 20 27	4 11 18 25	1 8 15 22 29
Friday	7 14 21 28	4 11 18 25	3 10 17 24 31	7 14 21 28	5 12 19 26	2 9 16 23 30
Saturday	1 8 15 22 29	5 12 19 26	4 11 18 25	1 8 15 22 29	6 13 20 27	3 10 17 24
Sunday	2 9 16 23 30	6 13 20 27	5 12 19 26	2 9 16 23 30	7 14 21 28	4 11 18 25

	JULY	AUGUST	SEPTEMBER	OCTOBER	NOVEMBER	DECEMBER
Monday	3 10 17 24 31	7 14 21 28	4 11 18 25	2 9 16 23 30	6 13 20 27	4 11 18 25
Tuesday	4 11 18 25	1 8 15 22 29	5 12 19 26	3 10 17 24 31	7 14 21 28	5 12 19 26
Wednesday	5 12 19 26	2 9 16 23 30	6 13 20 27	4 11 18 25	1 8 15 22 29	6 13 20 27
Thursday	6 13 20 27	3 10 17 24 31	7 14 21 28	5 12 19 26	2 9 16 23 30	7 14 21 28
Friday	7 14 21 28	4 11 18 25	1 8 15 22 29	6 13 20 27	3 10 17 24	1 8 15 22 29
Saturday	1 8 15 22 29	5 12 19 26	2 9 16 23 30	7 14 21 28	4 11 18 25	2 9 16 23 30
Sunday	2 9 16 23 30	6 13 20 27	3 10 17 24	1 8 15 22 29	5 12 19 26	3 10 17 24 31